CROSSROAD

Together Along the Way: Conversations inspired by the Directory for Catechesis

Hosffman Ospino and Theresa O'Keefe, editors.

The Crossroad Publishing Company

© 2021

Together Along the Way:
Conversations inspired by the
Directory for Catechesis

© 2021 by Hosffman Ospino and Theresa O'Keefe, editors.

ISBN: 978-0-824579-00-5

Cover Design by Eduardo Chumaceiro d'E.

The Crossroad Publishing Company
www.CrossroadPublishing.com

Crossroad, Herder & Herder, and the crossed C logo/colophon are
registered trademarks of The Crossroad Publishing Company.

All rights reserved. No part of this book may be copied, scanned, reproduced
in any way, or stored in a retrieval system, or transmitted, in any form or
by any means, electronic, mechanical, photocopying, recording, or otherwise,
without the written permission of The Crossroad Publishing Company.
For permission please write to rights@crossroadpublishing.com.

Library of Congress Cataloging-in-Publication Data
Available upon request.

Books published by The Crossroad Publishing Company may be
purchased at special quantity discount rates for classes and institutional use.
For information, please email sales@CrossroadPublishing.com.

Contents

Introduction
> p. 9

Horizons

1
What Faith and How to Educate For It?
Thomas H. Groome
> p. 15

2
Catechesis and the Community of Hope
Nathaniel Samuel
> p. 35

3
From Theology and Pedagogy to Practice: Building on Firm Foundations
Susanna Singer
> p. 57

4
Slow Catechesis: Liturgy, Popular Piety, and Beauty in the Directory for Catechesis
Timothy P. O'Malley

p. 79

5
Dialogue - Key to an Evangelizing Catechesis
Jane E. Regan

p. 99

6
Enfleshing Catechesis Through Embodied Space
Lakisha R. Lockhart

p. 117

Contexts

7
Antiracism and the 2020 Directory for Catechesis
Steffano Montano

p. 137

8
The Horizon and the Guiding Community
Theresa A. O'Keefe

p. 157

9
Catechesis and Digital Culture
Daniella Zsupan-Jerome

p. 175

10
Shaping a Meaningful Vision for Life in Today's World
Patrick R. Manning

p. 195

11
The Parish as a Vital Space of Catechetical Formation
Susan Bigelow Reynolds

p. 215

12

Lost in Cultural Translation: A Roadmap for Catechesis in a Culturally Diverse Church
Hosffman Ospino

p. 235

Contributors

p. 255

Introduction

The 2020 *Directory for Catechesis* (henceforth, *Directory*) is the third resource of its kind available to the Catholic catechetical community since the Second Vatican Council. The previous directories were published in 1971 and 1997. Directories offer direction. They are guides for the journey. Each directory seeks to respond to the emerging insights and concerns of a particular time in the years leading to it. Directories also elicit fresher forms of catechetical reflection. As the world changes, the church's efforts to catechize must adapt as well while remaining focused on the ultimate horizon, "the encounter with the Lord Jesus" (§56).

The *Directory* offers an overarching vision for catechesis in the global church and it does so by taking a necessary distance from the particularities of each society and each faith community. It speaks to many publics in various contexts. It may not feel immediately useful or directive to catechetical leaders and evangelizers on the ground. Rather than a trail map, the *Directory* is more like an atlas. It shows the relationship among parts and a view of the whole, yet it is not the instrument that a catechetical community would use primarily for planning specific sessions and programs.

This collection was conceived as a resource to help you make the trail map for you diocese, parish or school. It identifies essential themes from the *Directory* and names important contours that shape ecclesial life in the Unites States of America. As on any journey, when we have a good vision of the horizon in light of the context in which we live, we can better understand how to make a path to meet it. In the first part of the collection, *Horizons*, six authors take the long view, naming the goals of catechesis and the various means of travel—pedagogical, theological, and methodological—of meeting those goals. In the second part, *Contexts*, another six authors identify the twists, turns, obstacles and opportunities particular to the U.S. reality that determine how to make the path. All twelve writers have expertise in the field of catechesis as practitioners and catechetical scholars.

Catholics in the United States share our faith at a historical moment in which we are perhaps more intentionally aware about who we are culturally and racially in our society than ever before. As we make claims about our Christian discipleship and how we can better catechize, we also make important claims about our racial, ethnic, and cultural identities. How we name those claims matters. The authors of the essays in this collection use a variety of categories and formats to name ourselves and those communities to which we are accountable. You may agree or disagree with some of them. You may find them interesting and stimulating. We want you to join the conversation.

The title of the collection, *Together Along the Way*, evokes the story of the disciples on the road to Emmaus. They ask themselves "Were not our hearts burning within us while he was talking to us on the road, while he was opening the scriptures to us?" (Luke 24: 32). The disciples' question illustrates that the encounter with Christ happens not only at the end of our journey, but also along the way, in the speaking and listening. *Conversations Inspired by the Directory for Catechesis* reflects the conversational nature of this book. Each chapter ends with reflection questions and suggestions for further reading. We hope to inspire exiting conversations with the people you serve and those with whom you work. In fact, the writing process was the result of a sustained conversation among the authors. We read one another's chapters, offered feedback, and made references across the collection. We too are a community in conversation about catechesis, inspired by the *Directory*.

All the authors in this collection share the experience of being associated with the Boston College's PhD program in Theology and Education, either as faculty or as graduates. May this be an opportunity to express our gratitude and admiration to Thomas H. Groome and Jane E. Regan. Both served as mentors to all of the other contributors as each made his or her way through doctoral studies. Their scholarship, colleagueship and friendship sustain us as sojourners in the field of Religious Education. We hope that this collection honors the strong foundation they set down in each of us—and countless others—for religious education and catechesis in the United States.

The Editors

Horizons

1
What Faith and How to Educate For It?
Thomas H. Groome

What is the Christian faith for which we are to catechize and *how* might catechists do so effectively? There are no more foundational catechetical questions than these. Our response to the first question —*what* faith— must surely shape our response to the second, that we employ a pedagogy which, by God's grace, is likely to encourage the "desired learning outcome." Of course, as Paul well reminded, faith is always "the gift of God" (Ephesians 2:8) and yet, from our side of the divine/human covenant, our catechesis should be an effective instrument of God's grace.

Belief not Enough

Given the more recent history of our vital ministry, we cannot take for granted the wisest response to either of our two foundational questions. Indeed, for more than four hundred years now, from the Council of Trent (1545-1563) until the Second Vatican

Council (1962-1965), the church has generally taken-for-granted that the "faith" for which we are to catechize is constituted solely as *belief*, and belief especially in the dogmas and doctrines of the Catholic Church. The origins of this posture can be understood within the historical context of Trent; the Protestant Reformation had challenged many traditional Catholic beliefs and the church's reaction was to emphasize what we *believe* all the more.

The *Catechism of Trent* (also known as *The Roman Catechism*) was first published in 1566, and designated "for Priests"—presumed to be the chief catechists (Note that the 2020 *Directory for Catechesis*—henceforth, *Directory*—is explicitly addressed to the whole church as responsible for evangelization). Trent's Catechism became by far the most influential text in disseminating the Council's reforms; in many cultures, the priests preached on it every Sunday in a three-year cycle. It defined faith as "that by which we yield our unhesitating assent to whatever the authority of our Holy Mother the church teaches us to have been revealed by God." The text goes on to explain that any kind of questioning or doubt about church teachings reflects a *lack* of faith— even a sin against it. This tended to make *belief* the sum total of Christian faith and to be embraced out of obedience to the teaching authority of the church rather than by personal persuasion and toward relationship with Jesus Christ. Trent's insistence on faith as unquestioning *belief* in church teaching remained in place up until the Second Vatican Council, and is still in vogue among more traditionalist Catholics today.

With total emphasis on the beliefs of faith in place, the logical step for catechesis was simply to summarize those beliefs and have people memorize them. And this was precisely what the church did. From the *Catechism of Trent* there emerged the popular catechisms that were the standard for Catholic catechesis up until Vatican II. The most influential early popular texts were those by St. Peter Canisius (first published in 1555 and eventually translated into over 500 languages) and St. Robert Bellarmine (published 1598). These led on to the question-and-answer, easy to memorize popular catechisms such as the *Maynooth*, the *Baltimore*, the

Penny, and so on, all slight variations of each other (much of the *Baltimore Catechism* was borrowed from the *Maynooth Catechism*, which borrowed from *Butler's Catechism*, etc.)

Now, let us not be unduly critical of the question-and-answer catechisms; we stand, in large part, on the shoulders of "catechism Catholics." They gave Catholics a certain confidence that they "knew" their faith and could share it as called upon. Ask your grandparents a question like, "Who made the World" or "Why did God make you" and I'll wager that they will still be able to recite "the answer"—and *by heart* (reflecting personal ownership more than by rote). The catechisms honored one essential aspect of Catholic faith, namely to know, understand, and embrace its central beliefs.

Surely there is still need for Catholics to know and be able to recall "by heart" the core symbols of their faith. This would not be all 421 questions and answers in the original *Baltimore Catechism* (1885), but would include the commandments, the sacraments, the beatitudes, the Creeds, core prayers (Our Father, Hail Mary, Glory be etc.) and some central scripture quotes (e.g., John 3:16, Genesis 1:27). The assembling of such core beliefs should honor what Vatican II referred to as "the hierarchy of truths," and not to teach every aspect as equally central and "for the heart."

Such selectivity and highlighting of core beliefs was not reflected in the popular catechisms; for example, the *Baltimore Catechism* had eleven questions and answers on how to gain *indulgences*. By contrast, it had only one question on the resurrection of Jesus, simply noting that Easter Sunday was when Jesus rose from the dead but with no further catechesis on its centrality to Christian faith. And while recognizing that the Catechisms attempted to honor one aspect of faith, namely *belief*, this falls far short of the totality of Christian faith.

Christian Faith as a Whole Way of Life

Beginning with Vatican II and central to the three catechetical *Directories* since then (1975, 1998 and now 2020), the church and its catechesis has clearly returned to an understanding of faith as our whole way of life in the world. Beyond our beliefs, it includes the quality of our relationships with God and each other, and the moral commitments and virtues by which we are to live. Aquinas' proposal that the three great virtues of faith, hope and love are symbiotic suggests that faith, like love, is to engage all of one's mind, heart, and strength—people's very soul (see Mark 12:28-34). Or we might say that Christian faith is to engage the whole person, our *heads*, *hearts*, and *hands*, shaping how we *believe*, *belong*, and *behave* in our baptismal vocation to live as disciples of Jesus in a community of disciples and for God's reign in the world.

Vatican II began our return to such a holistic understanding of faith, summarizing its essence as "our free human response to God" and to the divine initiative in our lives (*Dignitatis Humanae*, § 10). The Council called all Christians to "the witness of a *living* and mature faith" (emphasis added and elaborated below) which "needs to prove its fruitfulness by penetrating the believer's entire life, including its worldly dimensions and by activating (people) toward justice and love, especially regarding the needy" (*Gaudium et Spes*, § 21).

Following the sentiments of Vatican II, and echoing the two previous Directories, the 2020 *Directory for Catechesis* continues to emphasize this holistic understanding of Christian faith. From the beginning and throughout, it insists that "Christian faith is, first of all, the welcoming of God's love revealed in Jesus Christ, sincere adherence to his person, and the decision to follow him" (*Directory*, § 18). It well notes the "cognitive dimension of the faith" (§ 80). Yet, Christian faith always demands much more than we typically mean by "belief"—commonly seen, at most, as an intellectual assent. Far beyond belief, the *Directory* insists that "faith implies a profound existential transformation" and is "to manifest at all levels of the Christian's existence" (§ 20). The *Directory* echoes often that "faith deserves to be known, celebrated, lived and turned into prayer" (§ 79).

Living Faith as Alive, Lived and Lifegiving

We already noted above that Christian faith is to engage the whole person, head, heart and hands —one's very soul. As such, faith includes believing, relating (with God and others), and behaving, all after "the way, truth and life" (John 14:6) as modeled by Jesus. As the *Directory* repeats often, Jesus must ever be the cornerstone of everything we teach, the model of *living* faith we are to propose. For example, "at the center of all catechesis is the person of Jesus Christ, living, present and active" (§ 169), ever calling disciples to *living* faith in his footsteps. We can further unpack *living* faith as faith *alive*, *lived*, and *life-giving*—for self, others and world.

Alive faith is to be fresh and vibrant, constantly renewing and deepening, a *gradual* journey (Pope Francis) that ever reaches into new horizons of faithfulness. *Alive* faith continues to grow and develop across the life-span until we finally rest in God. In his conversation with a Samaritan woman at a well (John 4), Jesus promised her that his Gospel would always be like "living water," much as "a spring of water gushing up to eternal life" (John 4:10, 14). Christians must return often to the fresh waters of Jesus' Gospel; otherwise, our faith can become as stagnant—which kills!

Lived faith. From the beginning of his public ministry, Jesus invited disciples to follow his way, to walk in his footsteps. He repeatedly prioritized *lived* faith as the measure of discipleship, and here we could pile on the quotes. For example, "Not everyone who says to me, 'Lord, Lord,' will enter the kingdom of heaven, but only the one who does the will of my Father in heaven" (Matthew 7:21). So, not the *confessing* but the *doing* is what makes faith real. As Jesus repeated often, in one way or another, "blessed are those who hear the word of God and obey it" (Luke 11:28). In an amazing moment when his mother and family came looking for him, Jesus declared that his family now are "those who hear the word of God and do it" (Luke 8:21). For Jesus, faith must get done.

Life-giving faith. Throughout his public ministry, it is amply clear that Jesus lived and taught a life-giving faith, a faith that would be salvific and liberating for oneself, for others, and especially for those most in need. Such life-giving faith was best symbolized in his teaching and praxis for the reign of God—the most utopian symbol imaginable. Living faith after the way of Jesus must contribute to his stated life-purpose as "for the life of the world" (John

6:51) and promote "life in abundance" for all (John 10:10). This translates into very concrete issues and struggles for social justice, like opposing racism, every form of prejudice and discrimination, and caring for our "common home" (Pope Francis)—the environment.

The Context Needed for Living Faith

Nurturing people in such holistic faith is an ontological task; it is to shape people's very *being* (Greek *ontos*)—not simply what they believe. For this reason, and to expand on the old African proverb, education-in-faith requires *a family in a village with a school*—taking village to mean parish or faith community and *school* pointing to the need for intentional and formal catechesis. To educate the very *being* of people in *living* faith as disciples of Jesus, requires first and foremost the context of Christian family and community. Of course, God's grace can "work" through all kinds of unlikely contexts, but, typically, nothing is more influential to becoming Christian than our primary socialization of home and parish. This wisdom is so well reflected in the pandemic-time experience recounted by Susan Reynolds in this collection. Her young daughters "had been catechized by their inclusion in the ritual life of our parish community" (and, I'm sure, by their Christian family context as well).

Regarding the need for Christian family and community for effective catechesis, the *Directory* is explicit and constant. It says at the outset, and repeats throughout, that Christian faith is "kindled, sustained, and transmitted only in the communion of ecclesial faith....together with the Church" (§ 21), with the latter functioning as "a family of families" (§ 226). Then regarding family, it explicitly states that "as a domestic church (echoing Vatican II) founded on the sacrament of marriage that also has a missionary dimension, the Christian family takes part in the Church's mission of evangelization and is therefore an agent of catechesis" (§ 231). It states often that parents are "above all the first catechists of their own children" (§ 124). Here the *Directory* echoes the commission that parents receive when their child is baptized: they are to be "the first teachers of their child in the ways of faith," with "first" meaning the most vital.

The Pedagogy Needed for Living Faith

Recognizing the central role of both family and parish community, yet there is ever need for "schooling" in Christian faith as well, for intentional catechesis that employs an effective pedagogy. This can be located in a parish program or a Catholic school, and, indeed, can flow over into the home for its intentional conversations of faith. What might be the distinctive features of such more formal educating-in-faith?

Here again, the *Directory* is quite explicit. We can summarize its proposed pedagogy as reflecting threefold tasks: a) it must engage the real lives and everyday experiences of the participants; b) it must give them ready and persuasive access to the truths, values, practices and wisdom of Christian faith and as relevant to their lives; and c) it is to encourage people to integrate these two sources—their everyday lives and Christian tradition—into *living* faith. Consistently, the *Directory* finds the primary warrant for such an engaging pedagogy in that of Jesus as reflected throughout his public ministry.

The *Directory* highlights that Jesus' favored approach was to begin with the realities and issues of people's lives. "In his proclamation of the Kingdom, Jesus seeks, encounters, and welcomes people in their concrete life situations" (§ 198). He engaged people's everyday lives by "starting from the observation of facts and experiences known to all" and then "prompts his hearers to ask questions and to begin an inner process of reflection" (§ 198). The *Directory* notes that Jesus' engaging of people's lived experience "shines through in the parables especially" (§ 198). And it issues a dire warning that "if catechesis neglects to correlate human experience with the revealed message, it falls into the danger of artificial juxtapositions or misunderstandings of the truth" (§ 199).

Then, into the midst of people's lives and experiences, Jesus taught his Gospel of God's reign "with authority" (Mark 1:22), inviting people to integrate their lives and the faith he was proposing. Through "a relationship of reciprocity and dialogue" he encouraged potential disciples to integrate the two sources—life and Gospel—into "life lived in openness and harmony with the work of God" (§§ 197-198). I will briefly describe such catechesis below as "bringing life to Faith and Faith to life." It is reflected, as the *Directory* signals, throughout Jesus' public ministry but nowhere more explicitly than in the pedagogy of the Risen Christ with the two disciples on the Road to Emmaus (Luke 24:13-35).

Following the lead of Pope Francis who often cites the Emmaus Road story as an example, the *Directory* constantly refers to the key posture for catechists toward their students as one of *accompaniment* (§ 113, § 135, etc.). And even as the Stranger "walked with them," note his pedagogical moves as well. He begins by inviting them to tell him of their own recent experience in Jerusalem, their story of what had happened to their beloved Jesus and likewise heard of their hope for a messiah who would set Israel free (v 21). Then into their own story and shattered vision, the Stranger recalls for them the whole faith tradition of their people for a promised messiah, but a suffering servant instead of a political one (v 26). Eventually, from their sharing a meal together, the two disciples recognize the Risen Christ Jesus in their midst, they come to *see* for themselves, whereupon he "vanishes from their sight" (v 31). Instead of continuing on to Emmaus, they return to Jerusalem to re-join the Christian community there in a life of *living* faith.

Note, too, that while the *Directory* says there are many expressions of Christian faith (scriptures and traditions, dogmas and doctrines, symbols and sacraments, etc.), yet "narrative language" is particularly effective pedagogically to access Christian faith because it engages the "affective, cognitive, (and) volitional" of people's lives (§§ 207-208). As on the Road to Emmaus, Jesus practiced and encouraged such narrativity in representing his Gospel.

Following on and inspired by what it perceives as the pedagogy of Jesus, the *Directory* states that "the work of the catechist consists in finding and drawing attention to the signs of God's action already present in the lives of persons" and from this "to present the Gospel as a transformative power for the whole of existence" (§ 179). Continuing to echo this placing in reciprocity of people's lived experience with Christian faith, it insists that "the methodology of catechesis must refer to the word of God and at the same time attend to the authentic demands of human experience" (§ 194). Because there should be compatibility "between method and content" (§ 194) *living* faith demands a pedagogy that engages people's lives with persuasion (§ 194)—not simply conveying information.

Catechesis, then, must bring about "the encounter of the word of God with the experience of the person" (§ 195). Again, "Human experience is integral to catechesis" precisely because "God speaks" to people through their own life experiences (§ 197). In sum, catechesis must set up "a relationship of reciprocity and dialogue" between people's own lives in the world—experience—and Christian faith (§ 197). After such integration, there is a place for memorizing; however, "the texts that are memorized must at the same time be taken in and gradually understood in depth in order to become a source of Christian life on the personal and community level" (§ 202).

Though all age levels deserve to be engaged by such a participatory catechesis, the need is all the more urgent for youth and young adults as they move developmentally into their own decision-making time by way of faith identity. As

Theresa O'Keefe well argues in her chapter in this collection, to educate youth and young adults into an enduring faith, the catechesis simply must connect and integrate with what truly matters to their lives. We need to teach Christian faith in compelling and persuasive ways so that young people can recognize for themselves and personally embrace it as valuable and meaningful for them.

Overall Recommendation

Given the holistic understanding of faith that is now deeply re-established in the consciousness of the church, the new *Directory for Catechesis*, like the two before it, calls for a pedagogy that engages the everyday realities, issues and themes of people's lives. Paulo Freire would say that its pedagogy is to engage people's own *realidad* and encourage their speaking their own word and reflecting critically upon those realities. We might image this as enabling people to attend to, reflect upon, and share their own stories and visions, the issues and hopes of their lives. Then into the midst of their lives, catechesis must give people ready and persuasive access to the great truths, values and wisdom of Christian faith—to its whole Story and inviting Vision.

Then, the pedagogy must encourage people to integrate these two sources, people's own stories and visions with the Story and Vision of Christian faith. To echo Bernard Lonergan who did such groundbreaking work on the dynamics of cognition, such integration must invite people to a knowing that reflects their own judgments and decisions. Catechetically, this amounts to encouraging participants to "see for themselves" the beauty and truth of this "greatest Story ever told" and to appropriate it into their own hearts, minds, and wills—into their souls. By God's grace, such a pedagogy is likely to dispose people to bring their lives to Christian faith and Christian faith to their lives—as *living* faith.

Questions for Conversation:
1 Recall for a few moments how you came by your own deep Christian faith. Who or what shaped it and how? Now, recognize what you might learn

for your catechesis now from your own catechetical story.

2 What adjustments might you need to make to embrace the *Directory's* sense of holistic faith and its recommended pedagogy that integrates people's lives with "the Gospel" and all toward *living* faith?

Recommended Readings:

James Bacik. *Saints: Celebrated and Unsung*. Maryknoll, NY: Orbis Press, 2021.

Thomas Groome. *Faith for the Heart*. New York: Paulist Press, 2019.

Anne Streaty Wimberly. *Soul Stories: African American Christian Education*. Nashville, TN: Abingdon Press, 2005.

2
Catechesis and the Community of Hope
Nathaniel Samuel

We cannot flourish without hope. Indeed, many of our most cherished stories from scripture remind of that fact. When the people of Israel came out of Babylonian exile, the prophet Isaiah (61:1-3) had a word of hope for them:

> The spirit of the Lord God is upon me,
>   because the Lord has anointed me;
> [the Lord] has sent me to bring good news to the oppressed,
>   to bind up the brokenhearted,
> to proclaim liberty to the captives,
>   and release to the prisoners;
> to proclaim the year of the Lord's favor,
>   and the day of vengeance of our God;
>   to comfort all who mourn;
> to provide for those who mourn in Zion—
>   to give them a garland instead of ashes,

the oil of gladness instead of mourning,
   the mantle of praise instead of a faint spirit.

These words were a balm of hope to a people who believed God had abandoned them—assuring of God's faithful agency and inviting them to serve God in loosing all "bonds of injustice" (Isaiah 58:6). Centuries later, Jesus would take up this mission as his own (Luke 4:18-21), healing the brokenhearted and bringing hope to the hopeless. He too summons us to commit to this mission; to be a community of hope!

The Gospel of hope is needed with urgency today. Many are hurting in our world, and all too often hope appears to be in short supply. The tragedies and losses associated with a global pandemic, the persistent specter of race-based violence on our streets, as well as a growing recognition of how entrenched structural racism is in society are just a few issues that have engendered deep feelings of despair, anger, disorientation and hopelessness.

Yet, Christian faith must lend hope even, and especially, within the most trying of circumstances.

Indeed, the *Directory for Catechesis* (henceforth, *Directory*) describes the Gospel as "*a principle of hope for the whole world and for the people of every time*" (§ 172, emphasis added). It reminds us that hope is born in our "living encounter with Christ" (§ 75). Furthermore, as bearers of this good news, the Christian community is the "*the community of hope lived and communicated*" (§ 28, emphasis added), and its catechists are hope's privileged expression or sign (§ 113). How do we continue Jesus' ministry of hope in our time and place in history? How do we live the *Directory's* lofty vision? What does it mean to have hope in our turbulent times, amidst stories and experiences of uncertainty, pain, survival and courage? How can catechesis serve the proclamation (and the living) of the gospel as a principle of hope for the world? How do we catechize the community for a faith that lends hope?

What is hope? What is it not?

First, what is hope and what is it not? Hope is often identified with optimism, but the Christian understanding is very different. Optimism relates to positive thinking. It is future-oriented, is rooted in human effort and in confidence in achieving a desired goal. It believes that good will always triumph over evil. In contrast, while hope shares this future orientation, it is not contingent on the realization of a coveted goal. Rather, hope sustains our daily life even while admitting to the *genuine possibility for failure*. It does not presume that good will always have the day—only that it will *ultimately* do so.

Bryan Massingale in his book, *Racial Justice and the Catholic Church* has reflected on this point in the context of the Black Church experience. He writes, "Authentic hope is neither illusory nor escapist. It looks squarely at the intransigence of evil; acknowledges the tragedy of loss and defeat; yet refuses to accept that evil, tragedy, and defeat will have the final say in human affairs" (p.148).

Hope assumes this horizon because, as the *Directory* reminds, it "springs from the Easter of Christ" (§ 426). It is an orientation of trust in the saving love of God through Jesus Christ, which motivates and sustains our life efforts and commits us to "work for a non-guaranteed future [even] in the face of formidable obstacles" (Massingale, p.147). Having hope is essential for sustaining us through the slow and often difficult work of justice; it keeps our hearts on an eternal horizon (§ 426). As Pope Francis writes in his encyclical *Fratelli Tutti*, hope

> speaks to us of something deeply rooted in every human heart, independently of our circumstances and historical conditioning. Hope speaks to us of a thirst, an aspiration, a longing for a life of fulfillment, a desire to achieve great things, things that fill our heart and lift our spirit to lofty realities like truth, goodness and beauty, justice and love.... Hope is bold; it can look beyond personal convenience, the petty securities and compensations which limit our horizon, and it can open us up to grand ideals that make life more beautiful and worthwhile. (§ 55)

Also of significance is that the practice of *lament* is essential for cultivating hope. Lament is a bridge from despair to hope. It is a crying out to God that does not necessarily resolve what gives us pain, but helps us carry that burden better, more sustainably and with greater agency—with hope.

The scriptures offer much evidence of the power of lament in this task. It comprises a significant genre in the Psalms (over one third) and the book of Lamentations. Take, for example, Psalm 3:

> O Lord, how many are my foes!
>> Many are rising against me;
> many are saying to me,
>> "There is no help for you in God."
> But you, O Lord, are a shield around me,
>> my glory, and the one who lifts up my head.
> I cry aloud to the Lord,
>> and [God] answers me from [God's] holy hill.
> I lie down and sleep;
>> I wake again, for the Lord sustains me.
> I am not afraid of ten thousands of people
>> who have set themselves against me all around.
> Rise up, O Lord!
>> Deliver me, O my God!
> For you strike all my enemies on the cheek;
>> you break the teeth of the wicked.

> Deliverance belongs to the Lord;
>> may your blessing be on your people!

The pain and struggle of the psalmist is very evident in these words. Walter Brueggemann writes in his book *Spirituality of the Psalms*, that lament provides a language for despair and disorientation (p.25). It breaks open the spaces where anguish may immobilize our faithful agency. It issues forth into hope. Embedded in the psalm are words of hope in God, who is a shield and the 'lifter of my head.' Indeed, as do so many of the psalms of lament, Psalm 3 ends as a cry of hope, summoning God's deliverance.

Lament serves as the bridge to hope because it renews our memory of the saving God of history, and ultimately the paschal mystery of Jesus Christ. It re-members God's promises and makes possible the journey through the void left by grief, loss or anguish.

A Catechesis of Hope

In light of this understanding of hope, here are two suggestions for attending to the hope-full vision of the *Directory*—for advancing a catechesis of hope amidst the social ills that confront our communities today. The first advocates for *spaces for lament*; the second for *cultivating social grace* in church and society.

Cultivate Spaces for Lament

Echoing *Gaudium et Spes*, the *Directory* describes the vocation of disciples of Jesus to "share the joys and the hopes, the griefs and the anxieties of the [people] of this age" (§ 319). The practice of lament has an integral place in the sharing of grief and anxieties, and in the cultivation of hope. Yet, as pointed out by Anne E. Streaty Wimberly in her essay in *From Lament to Advocacy*, the Christian Church is losing the practice of lament from its ritual life—it has subsided from preaching, music ministry, and catechesis. This is indeed unfortunate.

To be a community of hope we need to imagine and cultivate spaces for lament within our ritual life—spaces where persons can give voice to their pain and anguish and be supported to renewed agency. The psalms of lament are gracious companions in this task. Whether sung in liturgies, prayed, or employed as generative themes in sermons and faith-sharing groups, these psalms provide the narrative mirror wherein persons may reflect on their own situation within the psalms' metaphors and movements.

Catechesis, as an instrument of a "conscious and intimate encounter with the Redeemer of humanity" (§ 427) has a central place in this cultivation and renewal of hope. The *Directory* describes the catechist as "a witness of faith and *keeper of the memory of God*" (§ 113, emphasis added).

> Keeping this memory, reawakening it in others, and placing it at the service of the proclamation is the specific vocation of the catechist. The testimony of [their] life is necessary for the credibility of the mission. Recognizing [their] own frailty before the mercy of God, the catechesis does not cease to be the sign of hope for [others]. (§ 113)

It is of vital importance, therefore, that catechists lead people in encountering anew the promises of God memorialized in faith, with the aim of "strengthening [them] in hope" (§ 427). How might this look? As Thomas Groome writes in his chapter in this collection, Christian pedagogy needs to engage the everyday realities and issues of people's lives, inviting conversation with the hope-filled stories and visions of the faith. Using Psalm 3 as a generative point for reflection, small groups may be invited to reflect on such questions as: Given what is taking place in our communities at the moment, what do you hear in the psalm that resonates or challenges you? What is "rising against you" today? What meaning do you find in the words that God is "the one who lifts up my head"? How has God been a shield for you, or sustained you in the past? What/where may God be inviting our community today? What do you most hope for in life? Engaging memory, will and imagination in this way may not only invite critical reflection on life, but a renewed sense of hope and agency in the transition from pain.

Admittedly, opening faith formation to such powerful emotions as grief and loss is difficult. Keeping a space open for such stories is always challenging. As a start, it helps if catechetical leaders themselves risk openness with their own spiritual journey and witness, which may invite others to risk the same within the intimate context of small faith sharing groups. To be a sign of hope for others, as the *Directory* envisions, needs risking honesty and transparency regarding one's own struggle and triumphs in the faith journey, and wrestling together to discern God's presence within the dailiness and uncertainties of life. To be "keepers of the memory of God," we must be ready to give "reasons for [our] hope" (§ 261) and welcome others into the workings of grace in our own story.

Cultivate Social Grace

Another strategy for implementing the *Directory's* vision is perhaps an ironic one: Christian hope is cultivated in the midst of the struggle for justice, and not from the sidelines. Working for justice is something the *Directory* calls for repeatedly. Indeed, it spotlights the vulnerable and the marginalized as urgent recipients of a catechesis of hope (§ 267).

A significant reason for despairing in the face of the problems that confront our communities is the overwhelming magnitude, complexity and seeming intractability of contemporary social issues. The specter of an unfolding climate crisis, the pervasive presence of institutionalized racism, polarizing xenophobia, tragic inequities in wealth and income levels, widespread disparities in access to health, education, and other essential life services, and then a global pandemic, all may seem too much for any conscious person to bear, let alone to respond with some sense of agency. Moreover, these issues are entrenched at the structural level—on a level above the individual human person. Their deep historical roots may further lend the impression that resolution in the foreseeable future is illusory and futile.

The *Directory*'s summons to the work of justice is hardly contingent on what ails our society. Rather, we need to be even more thoughtful, analytical, courageous and wise about the workings of society and about our personal agency. One way in which the church has conceptualized the entrenched nature of our social ills is as *structural* or *social sin*, which pertains to what Kevin Ahern in his book

Structures of Grace describes as "the destructive effects of social structures in perpetuating, sustaining, and supporting situations of injustice and oppression."[1] Structural sin pinpoints the understanding that sin is not simply personal and private but has a social dimension—it inhabits the institutional relationships (structures) that accommodate life in community. While structures possess no moral agency of their own, they may be considered sinful because of the destructive and oppressive effects they have on human life and relationships.

Structural sin may seem abstract, but this is hardly the case. It congeals in the workings of institutions in tangible ways. By restricting certain behavior and providing opportunities and incentives for others, institutions (as social structures) shape the choices that human beings face in moral deliberation—often in devastating and sinful ways. As Daniel K. Finn reminds in *Consumer*

---

[1] Kevin Ahern, *Structures of Grace: Catholic Organizations Serving the Global Common Good* (Maryknoll, NY: Orbis Books, 2015), 32.

Ethics, they "can be described as sinful when their constrictive or enticive power—the restrictions, opportunities, and incentives [that] persons encounter—encourage morally evil actions."[2]

Perhaps an example may be in order. The racially segregated school systems that exist in many cities across the United States may be described as sinful because of the deleterious effects they have on the life outcomes of children—especially children of color. The systems shape the available options for schooling by providing opportunities and incentives for attending well-funded schools that are available only to some parents, while restricting many families to historically and tragically under-resourced school districts. Moreover, such sinful social structures are maintained and perpetuated *because* their enticive and constrictive forces often go unchallenged.

If catechesis is to help sustain the community of hope, then it must provide opportunities and

---

2 Daniel K. Finn, *Consumer Ethics in a Global Economy: How Buying Here Causes Injustice There* (Washington, DC: Georgetown University Press, 2019), 116.

resources for persons to identify the workings of structural sin. More importantly, it must also lead to creativity and agency in the cultivation of *social grace*, the necessary counterpoint and resistance to social sin. Social grace describes God's redeeming and sustaining presence within social structures. As with social sin, social grace is present in tangible ways. It works through the opportunities, constraints and incentives employed by social structures that orient human decision making towards creating a more just, equitable and sustainable world.

To live into the hopeful vision of the *Directory*, therefore, we must value church communities as "structures of grace" in the world, wherein social grace may be nurtured.

> Christian communities may be seen as collective embodiments, or structures of grace, in the ways in which their theological and spiritual commitments inspire them to fight against injustice, indifference, and what the Christian tradition has described as structural or social sin. (Ahern, p.130)

In this vision, formation in the community of hope must entail leading persons to re-imagine and exercise agency in naming and dismantling structural sin and building a more just society. Despite the seeming intractability of contemporary social ills, we can—by God's grace—imagine a way forward. We can discern practical opportunities, constraints and incentives on human behavior that foster a more just, equitable and sustainable world.

Suggestions

Here are a few ideas: First, the church community can be more intentional in educating about the intimate connection between faith and social engagement. Whenever a church community makes this connection it is creating space where social grace can be imagined and nurtured. Steffano Montano's thought-provoking chapter in this collection details how this may be done in the area of anti-racist catechesis—rooting antiracist work in the practice of Eucharist, reflecting on the faith stories of survival and resistance from Black and Brown Catholics, and committing to racial and religious identity development in students. Faith educators need to have ready responses for often-voiced concerns as: What does addressing racism have to do with the gospel? Why should our parish take on this issue? Responses are needed that recount God's providential care for the marginalized and oppressed of history, and that speak to the integral place of social action and justice in the Gospel. This also means, on another level, that contemporary issues of justice need more critical and sustained treatment from the pulpit—always a powerful source of formation.

Second, catechesis needs to provide opportunities and resources for persons to identify and become conscious of the workings of structural sin, and to build and support institutional embodiments of social grace. Many parishes today are forming small groups to reflect on themes of racial justice and its roots in white supremacy and privilege. For many this is a challenging time, but it is essential. It is something that the Black Church has had to do for generations! Working through these concepts is essential for gaining critical awareness and responsible agency as disciples. And there are many partnerships to be found and cultivated in this effort; partners both traditional (Christian social movements) and non-traditional (such as the Black Lives Matter movement) that we need to work with as we re-imagine the workings of social grace for today.

Third, we can re-affirm and re-commit to family catechesis as a primary agent of social grace and hope. The *Directory* rightly emphasizes the potential in family life for "profound" Christian initiation and formation, including an "awakening of the sense of God" and "education of the moral conscience" (§ 227). Recognizing that family catechesis is hardly ever systematic and structured, it insists on how deeply formative the ongoing witness and commitment to justice within the family as a unit can be. Children are not left out, as they "have the capacity to pose meaningful questions relative to creation, to God's identity, [and] to the reason for good and evil" (§ 236). So too are the young who have "great capacity to bring about renewal, to urge and demand consistent witness, to keep dreaming and coming up with new ideas" (§ 244). We can re-commit to family catechesis by imagining and integrating opportunities and incentives for practicing solidarity and right relationship with all creation into the routine of family life.

Finally, faith communities need to be honest about the ways in which they act unjustly and/or stifle agency for change. Much courageous soul-searching needs to take place. As a first step, we need to discern the various restrictions, opportunities and incentives that operate at organizational levels, but also in ministry and in parish workplaces that lead to persons being treated unfairly, inequitably and unjustly and stymie commitments to change. It is rightly said that charity begins at home; so too does justice!

The Community of Hope

The journey into the kind of critical hope that is needed today is undoubtedly challenging, but also indispensable. To be a community that proclaims and witnesses to the Gospel of hope in these turbulent times, we need to create catechetical opportunities where persons can engage their everyday realities and find spaces to lament, where they may reflect on the workings of structural sin—yet imagine and create opportunities for social grace, and where they may engage anew the hope-filled Christian story and vision. Building the community of hope must also, and ultimately, begin with the family that nurtures the social agency of the young (and not so young) as part of its rhythm of life.

The *Directory* beckons us to be this community of hope, a living reality that embodies God's abiding presence in the world. As the prophet Isaiah did for the people of Israel, so too can the Christian community be a balm of hope in the world, assuring God's faithful agency and inviting commitment in undoing all bonds of injustice. I can imagine no more urgent, or worthwhile, commitment today.

Questions for Conversation:

1 What resources does your church community offer that help families to reflect and create daily practices around issues of social justice, social sin and social grace? Can you imagine possibilities for creating brave spaces for lament among existing ministries, or through new ones?

2. The issue of racism was used to illustrate the workings of social sin and grace above, but the analysis can be extended to other contemporary issues such as climate change, poverty and the pandemic. What experiences have you had with discussing such issues in catechetical settings? What questions or concerns have arisen? How would you imagine leading a conversation on social sin and social grace around any of these issues?

Recommended Readings:

Richard Lennan and Nancy Pineda-Madrid, eds. *Hope: Promise, Possibility and Fulfillment*. New York: Paulist Press, 2013.

Bryan Massingale. *Racial Justice and the Catholic Church*. Maryknoll, NY: Orbis Books, 2010.

Anne E. Streaty Wimberly, Nathaniel D. West and Annie Lockhart-Gilroy, eds. *From Lament to Advocacy: Black Religious Education and Public Ministry*. Nashville: Wesley's Foundery Books, 2020.

3
From Theology and Pedagogy to Practice: Building on Firm Foundations
Susanna Singer

Responding to a document from another Christian tradition feels a little like walking around someone else's living room. As a religious educator in the Episcopal Church and a priest for thirty years, I am delighted to have this opportunity and I promise to try not to knock over any furniture! My insights about the 2020 *Directory for Catechesis* (henceforth, *Directory*) spring from long experience in parish, cathedral, diocesan, and seminary settings, supported by my theological education in the Jesuit tradition. I am convinced that our churches have a great deal of common theological and ecclesiological ground from which to reflect together and even collaborate on the crucial ministry of catechesis. Building such ecumenical connections is especially important in the challenging context of North America today.

The new *Directory* provides an overview of principles for catechesis and formation in the

Roman Catholic Church worldwide. Its 30,000 feet perspective presents both challenges and opportunities for leaders who are responsible for designing and implementing catechesis on the ground. The principal challenge is that such a document cannot provide the kind of detail needed to create practical and specific strategies for particular local settings. The corresponding opportunity is that the *Directory* sets out in systematic ways theological and pedagogical principles that serve as the foundation for local approaches to these crucial ministries. It invites religious educators to use the pedagogical principles set forth and to build upon the theological foundation laid, in order to create coherent, effective, and fully inculturated practices of evangelism, catechesis and formation.

Theology and Pedagogy

A careful exploration of the theology and pedagogy of the *Directory* enables religious educators to avoid some common pitfalls in designing local catechetical frameworks: a rush to find novel programmatic "solutions" to perceived problems; an overly hidebound (by contrast) reliance on tried and true strategies; or a piecemeal approach that lacks coherence across generations and other groups within a community of faith. By starting with the principles laid out in the *Directory*, religious educators can make design decisions and programmatic choices that are coherent, reflective, and above all theologically sound. The *Directory* provides a yardstick for developing holistic catechetical approaches, integrated across the life-cycle of individuals and throughout the shared life of the Christian community. It does so primarily through its own integration of theology and pedagogy.

An Integrated Approach
The new *Directory* binds theology and pedagogy tightly and coherently together. Its strongest theological emphases are on revelation and incarnation (§ 14). It therefore places *kerygma*—the revelation of God's unfolding plan of salvation—at the center of catechesis. Though one weakness of the *Directory* is that it never explicitly defines that core

term, it is clear that *kerygma* is the ligature between evangelization and catechesis. Its central place in the *Directory* points towards catechesis that is always sharing the good news. This key theological and pedagogical move affirms *kerygma* as the heart of what the *Directory* repeatedly references as "the divine pedagogy," understanding God's self-revelation as profoundly educational in nature: "the great educational work of God" (§ 157). The Trinitarian divine nature manifests God's continuing creative presence in history, brings human salvation to fulfillment through the life, death, and resurrection of Jesus Christ, and empowers existential transformation through the work of the Holy Spirit (§ 12).

Without downplaying the importance of doctrine or tradition, the *Directory* proposes that *kerygma* is the theological foundation upon which catechesis is built (§ 59). Its Christ-centered "divine pedagogy" builds on incarnational theology to emphasize the need for contextual and dialogical approaches to catechesis (§ 58, § 60). It calls religious educators to move away from purely content-based and programmatic approaches towards the creation of integrated catechetical "ecosystems," attentive and responsive to the gifts, concerns, and needs of particular groups and contexts. It encourages catechists to draw upon the whole life of both the individual Christian and the community of faith, to develop mature, reflective Christian practitioners.

The *Directory* sets this high bar for integrated practices of evangelization, catechesis, and formation because *kerygma* calls all Christians to bear witness to the good news. The ministries of catechesis and formation are firmly linked to the church's "essential mission" of evangelization (§ 28). Catechesis and formation must equip ordinary Christians to evangelize: to re-present and mirror the divine life in their own (§ 58). Ideally, each Christian life makes Jesus Christ a living presence in the world, inviting people to respond in faith and build a developing relationship with God in Christ within a community of Christian believers, through the power of the Holy Spirit (§ 23). What kind of challenges to this bold catechetical goal are found in today's North American context?

The Contemporary North American Context: Challenges and Responses

Postmodern Epistemology

The postmodern mind-set that is broadly prevalent in early twenty-first century North America represents a significant break with the rationalism of late modernity. It embraces individualism, skepticism, and a lack of trust in historical institutions. It repudiates reason as the sole valid way to comprehend the world, and is correspondingly open to understanding truth as multiform and mediated most credibly through personal experience, story, art, and relationships. The *Directory* acknowledges the "complex reality" of this contemporary mind-set and insists that effective catechesis involves a careful reading of these signs of the times (§§ 319-320).

In order to present Christian faith as a credible, life-giving, and attractive possibility today, the church must take seriously the *Directory's* encouragement to place genuine relationships, beauty, mystery, and personal holiness at the center of catechesis and formation, rather than leading with rational propositions, doctrines, and traditions. This should lead to strategies that help developing Christians engage with salvation history, doctrine, and tradition through conversation and reflection, rich and reflective experiences of worship, Bible study that connects Scripture to life, and shared experiences with their peers that combine prayer, contemplation, and action for justice. Such imaginative, relational strategies build on classical catechumenal principles while responding faithfully to the new ways that the perennial human hunger for truth and integrity of life is manifested today.

A Post-Christendom Context

Another significant shift in the background conditions for evangelization, catechesis, and formation is that the social and cultural supports for Christian faith and life that existed even in the recent past have significantly eroded. We live in a pluralistic, post-Christendom world in which religious affiliation has become a choice. A major challenge for religious educators is therefore to find compelling ways to invite people into the life of faith, into relationship with God in Jesus Christ, and into the lifelong work of developing a religious identity that will enable them to live with integrity as Christians in a pluralistic culture.

Personal witness and generous autobiographical sharing by mature Christians, action for justice that is clearly inspired by faith, practical solidarity with those left behind by increasing inequality, public worship that accessibly crosses boundaries into the secular world and presents the beauty of Christian faith and life in vivid and contemporary ways—all these are effective evangelizing strategies for this time. The *Directory* emphasizes that "the whole Christian community is responsible for the ministry of catechesis" (§ 111) and affirms a relational pedagogy in which catechists manifest an attitude of compassion, respect, and "unconditional acceptance" (§ 135 c).

Happily, the strategies I propose to address postmodernity and pluralism also have the potential to re-evangelize and form those already Christian and seeking to deepen their life of faith. In the

Episcopal Church, I have observed the evangelizing and formational power of personal witness by the Most Reverend Michael Curry, trusted and charismatic leader and our first African-American Presiding Bishop. He uses his role as a public religious figure as well as his ministry as the Episcopal Church's chief catechist to articulate a vivid and compelling picture of what he calls "the Jesus movement." Through public preaching (for example, at the wedding of Prince Harry and Meghan Markle), in diocesan revival events, and in his popular 2020 book *Love is the Way: Holding Onto Hope in Troubled Times*, Presiding Bishop Curry articulates a vivid relationship with Jesus Christ. He draws on autobiography and story to make the *kerygma* come alive for ordinary people, many of who are not Christians. A carefully designed curriculum (*The Way of Love*) offers our congregations ways to make catechetical and formational use of his witness.

In response to Presiding Bishop Curry's passion for evangelism, the Episcopal Church has substantially increased its programmatic support for this ministry at the denominational level. New initiatives promote intentional dialogical interaction through digital media in order to form ordinary Christians as evangelists by inviting them to share their faith, inspiring them with personal examples of how to do this in everyday encounters, and describing the impact such witness has on those around them.

All Christians are Theologians

As well as effective evangelization, the post-Christian nature of contemporary North American culture demands catechesis and formation that foster the capacity for theological reflection in all Christians. We need better catechesis than socialization into received religious practices, uncritical reception of doctrine, and affiliation with an ecclesial community. Our goal should be to foster Christians' capacity to integrate faith and life, and to represent Christ in credible and attractive ways to their neighbors. As Jane Regan highlights in her chapter in this collection, this calls for catechesis that asks Christians to reflect on everyday dilemmas and choices in light of the church's teachings. It calls for support from the church as Christians navigate the complex relationship between their Christian identity and the many other identities that they inhabit in the world: as citizens, consumers, family members, employees (or employers), taxpayers, and participants in public and political life. In her chapter in this collection, Susan Reynolds discusses the local and geographical networks in which the parish is embedded, and names these as loci of formation. I claim that both individual and corporate expressions of faith must navigate the challenges posed by the multi-faceted nature of social identity, as well as contributing to the social goods that are created in community.

Developing this capacity for theological and hermeneutical reflection in all Christians (§ 196) is crucial given the issues with which North America is currently grappling: systemic racism and other oppression, deep-rooted social and economic inequalities, a historically exploitative relationship with the natural world, and the long shadows cast by colonialism and white supremacy. Churches have long been party to, and on too many occasions have tacitly or actively supported, a *status quo* that has perpetuated oppression for many. It is essential to equip Christians to reflect theologically on how their faith in Jesus Christ relates to historical and current social and ecclesial practices that are painful to acknowledge and contemplate. Ordinary Christians today need to become theologians of their own lives within this challenging context. The incarnational, relational, and contextual pedagogy that arises out of the theology in the *Directory* offers the church valuable tools with which to form such theologically reflective Christians.

I have recently experienced the power of this kind of formation in an ecumenical setting, as I led one of several study groups bringing together members of my own parish and a neighboring Roman Catholic parish. We undertook ten sessions of in-depth study of the history of racism in the US, using the *Sacred Ground* curriculum developed by the Episcopal Church. Drawing on the strengths of both of our traditions, our shared theological commitments, and our personal experiences and stories resulted in rich ecumenical formation that is calling both communities of faith to shared action in our city.

Fully Contextual Evangelization, Catechesis, and Formation?

The *Directory's* theological emphasis on relationship with God in Christ brings with it the pedagogical emphases already noted: on beauty and imagination, memory and autobiography, story and community as means through which faith is effectively formed. I believe that by placing these dimensions of faith formation at the center of its pedagogy, the *Directory* will help the church respond to the multiple social and cultural contexts of North America. Relational, story-centered, imaginative catechesis enables the particular gifts and needs of local communities to shape formational strategies that are fully inculturated.

Despite this commitment, the *Directory* remains ambivalent about contextual catechesis. While expressing respect for culture as the place where the Spirit is continually at work "in the common experience of humanity" (§ 42), it also articulates concern about some dimensions of contemporary cultural life. The expressed need to "evangelize culture in order to inculturate the Gospel" (§ 43), results in catechetical proposals that are limited in their constructive engagement with particular contemporary cultural contexts. In contrast to the call for a risky embrace of mutually critical correlation between faith and culture, made by theologian David Tracy in his classic 1981 text *The Analogical Imagination: Christian Theology and the Culture of Pluralism*, the correlation articulated in the *Directory* too often remains a one-way street.

The *Directory* certainly emphasizes attending to and respecting the specific contexts in which the ministries of evangelization, catechesis, and formation are carried out today. Its examples of "catechesis in situations of pluralism and complexity" highlight many of the challenges summarized above, and attend to urban and rural contexts, traditional and local cultures, and popular piety (§§ 320-342). With regard to popular piety, however, I believe the church must not only attend to its expression among "the simple and poor" (§ 337), but recognize and honor examples of personal piety which do not neatly fit into ecclesial categories. Sociologist of religion Elizabeth Drescher, in her 2016 text *Choosing Our Religion*, presents attempts by postmodern adults to connect with transcendence and personal meaning outside the boundaries of the church. It behooves the church to take these cultural expressions of piety seriously, and to attend more closely to the piety of ethnically specific communities.

The *Directory* presents Jesus' teaching ministry as the foundational example of relational catechesis that respects the world in which it takes place (§§ 198-200). But while highlighting communities and families as the most effective pedagogical *loci* for catechesis and formation, the *Directory* seems reluctant to entertain the possibility that the Spirit might be at work in the diversity of family and relational structures currently developing in North America. By privileging traditional family structures and referring to non-traditional families and relationships as "complex and problematic," "marked by wounded love," and "irregular" in nature (§§ 233-4), the *Directory* belies its commitment to contextually sensitive accompaniment, listening, and understanding. It implies that evangelization, catechesis, and formation can serve only corrective functions in relation to these emerging patterns of human relationship. It is disappointing to note the inconsistency between this aspect of the *Directory*, and its emphasis elsewhere on the fruitfulness of attending closely to contextual factors and respecting them as potential arenas of divine grace.

Holistic Baptismal Identity

Despite these limitations and ambiguities, the theology and pedagogy set forth in the *Directory* support and promote necessary changes in the nature and form of evangelization, catechesis, and formation for today's North American context. In the new picture that emerges, the purpose of catechesis shifts from making good ecclesial Catholics to forming Catholic Christians who are able to live out faith coherently and reflectively in a pluralistic world, supported by their ecclesial community. The key skill to be developed in ordinary Christians is the capacity to interpret life through a Christian lens.

Therefore, for religious educators in the parish and the diocese, a holistic catechetical approach is needed, building on the theological grounding of the *Directory*, and making use of contextually specific pedagogical strategies. One such strategy will involve making intentional use of "the Christian community as the primary agent of catechesis" (§ 218). Others will involve crafting ways to support Christians as they constantly cross the boundaries between church and culture. In practice, this will require attending carefully to the formational value of preaching, teaching skills of theological reflection and incorporating them into all areas of parish life, and spotlighting committed Christian living wherever it is found.

The Episcopal Church has created (on a denominational rather than worldwide scale) strategies for Christian formation within a similar theological and pedagogical framework to that set forth in the *Directory*. Our ecclesial tradition also emphasizes theologies of revelation and incarnation, embraces holistic formational strategies, values historical models of catechesis, and supports baptismal identity lived out in the world. Two current Episcopal Church initiatives demonstrate how Roman Catholic religious educators might respond to the call of the *Directory* to renew the ministries of evangelization, catechesis, and formation at the local level.

The Episcopal Task Force for Faith Formation and Ministry of the Baptized recently developed a comprehensive resource on the characteristics and milestones of developing faith, together with strategies for formation appropriate to different stages of the journey of faith. *A Christian Life of Faith: Signs and Thresholds Along the Way* offers a developmental framework for lifelong Christian formation that integrates faith and contextual experience, equipping Christians for faithful living.

Similarly, *Baptized for Life* provides training for catechists and resources to help Christians discern and live out their baptismal identity and ministry. Its purpose is "identifying, embracing, and sustaining each person's Christian vocation." While it incorporates training designed to revive the classic catechumenate and revitalize formation for traditional milestones such as Confirmation, it principally aims to assist Christians in living out their faith in today's world. It encourages a holistic understanding of formation and emphasizes community as the primary place where skills in theological reflections are strengthened for ordinary Christians. Its methodology emphasizes "structured reflection upon experience of worship, scripture, and service in the light of the ongoing history of salvation." It brings people together for prayer, study, and conversation, supported by mentors, so that personal stories contribute to the story of the larger community of faith and God's evolving mission.

My own experience of developing approaches to evangelization, catechesis, and formation over many years has convinced me that without strong theological and pedagogical foundations, and without careful and respectful attention to context, such efforts will be piecemeal at best. I am encouraged by the ways in which the new *Directory* clearly points Roman Catholic religious educators in the direction of holistic, theologically integrated pedagogy. I am left with an eager curiosity about how the relational, incarnational, and contextual approach to evangelization, catechesis, and formation that is presented in the *Directory* will be realized. Above all, I am inspired by the way the *Directory* opens up possibilities for ecumenical collaboration, and the building of catechetical partnerships between Roman Catholics, Episcopalians, and other Protestant churches that share similar theological foundations.

Questions for Conversation:

1. As you think about practices of catechesis and formation in your local setting, which of the particular elements presented in the *Directory* (relationships, imagination, story and experience, context) will be most fruitful for your community of faith to explore and strengthen?

2. When you reflect on the *Directory's* call to attend to the whole life of the gathered Christian community as the *locus* of catechesis and

formation, which aspects of life in your own faith community present exciting possibilities for more holistic approaches?

Recommended Readings:
Ellen Bruckner, Kate Gillooly, Lisa Kimball, Julie Lytle, Deborah Bressoud, Sharon Ely Pearson, Tina Pickering, Melissa Rau, Vickey Garvey, Alexizandria Link, and James McKim. *A Christian Life of Faith: Signs and Thresholds along the Way*, 2020. Available online.

Baptized for Life: An Episcopal Discipleship Initiative. Virginia Theological Seminary https://baptizedforlife.org

4
Slow Catechesis: Liturgy, Popular Piety, and Beauty in the *Directory for Catechesis*
Timothy P. O'Malley

As dawn arrived on a warm June morning, my family stood outside the doors of the Pantheon with other pilgrims in Rome, awaiting entrance into the church for the feast of Pentecost. The Pantheon—a Roman temple consecrated as a Catholic church in the seventh century—is perhaps best known for the oculus or opening at the top of the dome. On the feast of Pentecost, at the conclusion of Mass, the firefighters of Rome drop thousands of rose petals through the oculus of the Pantheon to the delight of the gathered pilgrims. After two hours of waiting, Mass began. Having earned a seat in the very front because of our pre-dawn arrival, we did not notice the thousands of pilgrims behind us, crowding into the Pantheon. Thousands more had gathered in the Pantheon's piazza, hoping for a glimpse of the festivity inside.

At the conclusion of Mass, the eyes of all the pilgrims gazed heavenward toward the oculus. The first rose petal gently floated to the ground. As the recession of prelates and priests began, tens of thousands of rose petals began to fall from the oculus. The floor of the Pantheon was covered with an inch of fragrant rose petals. There were audible gasps, proclamations of beauty on the part of an assembly who rivaled the many languages of that first Pentecost in Acts. Those in the piazza, who remained outside the church, clapped their hands as the last rose petals floated to the floor of the nave. Even our two-year old toddler, having spent four hours in the Pantheon against his wishes, irrupted with joy.

Few of us will have the opportunity to be present at the Eucharistic liturgy at the Pantheon in Rome. And yet, as those involved in the ministry of catechesis in the 21st century, the festive playfulness of this Pentecost ritual is worth considering. The problem of disaffiliation—as described by Theresa O'Keefe in her chapter in this collection —is best counteracted not through an overly intellectualized re-proposal of Catholicism. Rather, catechesis must turn to the festive slowness of liturgical celebration, popular piety, and beauty. The 2020 *Directory for Catechesis* (henceforth, *Directory*) is an invaluable resource as we reconsider the very nature of catechesis for our age, an opportunity to re-propose to the human person the saving gift of festive inefficiency.

The Slow Pedagogy of Liturgical Festivity

In the academy, the language of disenchantment has become the privileged way of explaining secularization and thus disaffiliation. Once upon a time, religion was easy to practice because the world was enchanted. With the rise of technology and an almost idolatrous respect for the scientific method, we no longer perceive a world infused with the grandeur of God. The moon is just the moon, not part of the heavenly spheres whose primordial vocation is to praise God.

This narrative of disenchantment tells but part of the story. After all, enchantment has not gone away. Watch an iPhone commercial where you are invited to bend the knee before a device that promises both perfect communion and an authentic encounter with reality. Residents of the United States keep vigil outside of Apple stores—our temples of technological promise—before the release of a new device. We remain as enchanted as ever, except our objects of devotion have shifted. The market has colonized the religious imagination, proposing a world of infinite possibility mediated through consumer products.[1]

The market's charm is different from the ritual enchantment of Catholicism's festivals. For one, the market is dominated by work rather than festivity or leisure. The vigil outside of the iPhone store, awaiting the advent of the new device, is reliant upon processes of production. The consumer purchases the iPhone, Apple profits, and the consumer market grows. The Apple device is enchanted—almost like the Eucharist—but not permanently. When one brings the device home, it is immediately antiquated. After Apple proclaims the

[1] See Eugene McCarraher, *The Enchantments of Mammon: How Capitalism Became the Religion of Modernity* (Cambridge, MA: Harvard University Press, 2019) and Brett T. Robinson, *Appletopia: Media Technology and the Religious Imagination of Steve Jobs* (Waco, TX: Baylor University Press, 2013).

advent of the latest product, the once enchanted device is thrown into the trash heap. The human person is thereby formed into an impossible restlessness, where nothing is permanent except the insatiability of consumer desire. Acceleration and speed are identifying markers of this consumer and digital culture, and rapid innovation is necessary for survival.[2]

Catholicism proposes to humanity an alternative way of being human, grounded in the festival playfulness of liturgical celebration. Liturgical prayer is playful because it has no other end than placing the human person in the presence of God by inviting us to assume a posture of praise and adoration. To pray in the liturgy is to enter a world that we did not create, a festive space that it takes time to inhabit. The Catholic philosopher Josef Pieper writes that festivity—even though involving

---

2   See Harmut Rosa, *Social Acceleration: A New Theory of Modernity*, trans. Jonathan Trejo-Mathys (New York, NY: Columbia University Press, 2013), 1-32.

activity—is marked by a contemplative posture.³ We take the time to celebrate a feast not as a break from the workaday world but as the most authentic expression of what it means to be a creature who is made for self-gift.

Think back to the rose petals on Pentecost Sunday. There is nothing about those petals dropped from the roof of the Pantheon that is in the least productive or efficient. Those roses could have been sold for a profit to couples canoodling in dimly lit Italian piazzas. Certainly, those who waited outside the Pantheon might have made better use of their time.

And yet, the liturgy is not dominated by a concern with efficiency. Liturgical prayer takes the time to invite each person into a festive narrative of salvation. Byung-Chul Han proposes that:

> The religion of Christianity is to a large extent narrative. Festivals such as Easter, Whitsun

---

3   Josef Pieper, *In Tune with the World: A Theory of Festivity*, trans. Richard and Clara Winton (South Bend, IN: Saint Augustine's Press, 1965), 17-18.

[Pentecost] and Christmas are key narrative moments within an overall narrative which provides meaning and orientation. Every day is given a narrative tension, is made meaningful, by the overall narrative. Time itself becomes narrative, that is, meaningful. Capitalism lacks narrativity. It does not narrate anything…it merely counts…It deprives time of all meaningfulness. Time is profaned, reduced to labour time. Thus, all days resemble each other.[4]

The liturgy, therefore, invites us to take time to be inefficient. For it is through this inefficiency, committing ourselves to religious practices that shape us over years rather than minutes, that we begin to participate in the redeeming work of God.

---

[4] Byung-Chul Han, *The Disappearance of Rituals: A Topology of the Present*, trans. Daniel Steuer (Medford, MA: Polity Press, 2020), 44.

A Slow Catechesis: Liturgy, Popular Piety, and Beauty

The *Directory for Catechesis* invites catechetical leaders to learn a form of catechesis that is festively slow. The *Directory* proposes this form of catechesis through attention to the liturgy, popular piety, and beauty.

Catechists and religious educators alike have often misunderstood the language of liturgical celebration. Influenced by certain ritual theorists of the 20th century, religious educators and liturgists treated the liturgy as an aesthetic and symbolic language for presenting the otherwise abstract teachings of the Church. The *Directory* provides a subtle correction to this misunderstanding of the language of liturgical prayer:

> Catechesis…educates the believer in the attitudes that the Church's celebrations require: joy for the festive quality of celebrations, a sense of community, attentive listening to the word of God, confident prayer, praise and thanksgiving, awareness of signs and symbols (§ 82).

Notice that the *Directory* presents dispositions or capacities required for fruitfully celebrating the liturgy. Liturgical catechesis has as its *telos* not the mastery of information but developing a festive disposition. This festive disposition cannot be explained or discovered through speech alone. It takes practice, commitment to a form of life where one learns to dwell in the presence of God.

For example, each morning in the Liturgy of the Hours, the Christian marks her lips with the sign of the cross. During this ritual action, the believer cries out, "O Lord, open my lips, and my mouth shall declare your praise" — a passage taken from Psalm 51. The act of crossing one's lips is not immediately fruitful — even if it is accompanied by a brilliant interpretation. Taking up a posture of adoration before God, of letting one's entire discourse become praise, is the slow project of a lifetime.

In paragraph 98 of the *Directory*, the Church proposes for this reason a process of liturgical formation that unfolds slowly or gradually. Mystagogy—the privileged mode of post-baptismal catechesis—presumes that the Christian is engaged in regular practices of liturgical prayer. The person is attuned in this practice, slowly learning to see how the rites of the Church make possible our participation in the narrative of salvation. The believer becomes proficient in both contemplating and using the signs of the liturgy in prayer. This mystagogical catechesis is the project of a lifetime in which we slowly discover "...the awareness that the believers' existence is gradually transformed by the mysteries celebrated" (§ 98).

Liturgical catechesis, therefore, cannot be reduced to explaining the rites of the Church but must take on a certain contemplative and thereby festive dimension where we wondrously learn what it means to be an adorer of the living God. The liturgy is a source for all catechesis precisely because of its festive, slow, and contemplative nature (§ 95). The *Directory* does not return to the naïve clashes of old where catechists used the liturgy in a didactic manner, and liturgists proclaimed with unique hubris that all catechesis can be accomplished exclusively in the liturgical act. Liturgy is catechetical because it ensures that the Christian life including doctrinal instruction is "being oriented toward bring to life the experience of God's love" (§ 95).

As I have written in *Divine Blessing: Liturgical Formation in the R.C.I.A.*, this means that the liturgical rites, texts, as well as sacramental signs and symbols should be incorporated into every act of catechesis. The Incarnation, of course, may be taught through reference to the various councils of the Church. But the language of these Councils often lacks the imagery, the emotional appeal, that the digital native requires in the educative act (cf. *Directory*, § 363). The iPhone sells not because of its technical specifications but because of its hold upon the consumer imagination. The images of the liturgy function in a similar way, no longer presented as abstract thought but possessing a narrative hold on life. The collect or opening prayer of the Feast of the Annunciation is a poetic performance of the enfleshment of the Word. God emptied Himself, experiencing the fullness of the human condition in his conception in the womb of the Blessed Virgin. Those of us who confess faith in Jesus Christ as fully God and fully human — the collect prayer poetically presents — are to become partakers or participants in this mysterious exchange of love. To become divine is not a matter of seizing or grasping power but the mundane commitment to the giving of oneself unto the end in love. This collect prayer is a poetic and festive contemplation of the meaning of the Incarnation, leading the praying person to wonder, delight, and a new posture toward existence.

The liturgy, of course, does not encompass the fullness of the Church's public prayer. Slow catechesis, according to the *Directory*, is also related to popular piety. In the 20th century popular Catholicism or piety was dismissed by those interested in liturgical renewal, understood as conflicting with the Church's public prayer. The *Directory* corrects this false assumption of the 20th century in paragraphs 336-342. Popular piety is the fruit of a slow inculturation of the Gospel in time and space closely connected to the liturgical rites of the Church. Quoting from the text:

> Popular piety celebrates the mysteries of the life of Jesus Christ, above all his passion, venerates with tenderness the Mother of God, the martyrs and saints and prays for the deceased. It is

expressed through the veneration of relics, visits to shrines, pilgrimages, processions, the *via crucis*, religious dances, the rosary, medals, and other exercises of individual, family, and community piety. This, 'in the secularized environment in which our peoples live, continue to be a grandiose confession of the living God who acts in history, and a channel of the transmission of the faith,' almost constituting a reserve of faith and hope for a society that is losing its reference to God (§ 338).

Popular piety is a public manifestation that Jesus Christ has entered the history of a neighborhood or community and that festive time is the vocation of the human person. Festivals and processions, including dropping rose petals from the roof of the Pantheon, is not something that we progress beyond. They provide a source of stability for those who are on the margins of the Church, the disaffiliated who may have no other access to ecclesial life than in a procession during *Mardi Gras*, the feast of Our Lady of Guadalupe, or *Corpus Christi*. These acts of popular piety are often the religion of the poor and thus provide a critique of a certain market economy concerned exclusively with production and thereby efficiency.

The *Directory*'s attention to both beauty and art is also related to a slow, contemplative approach to catechetical formation. Beauty is first catechetical, according to the document, because of the nature of divine revelation. In both the Old and New Testaments, the glory of God is made manifest through material signs. And yet, our recognition of this beauty takes time. We must enter the feast where through contemplating beauty in the Word of God, as well as in contemporary art, we discover "sentiments of joy, pleasure, tenderness, fullness, meaning, thus opening us to the transcendent" (§ 109). All art, including that which is found in the liturgy, is integral to this formation into an aesthetic and contemplative disposition. The *Directory* comments that "art can have the merit of opening the person to the language of the senses, helping him not to remain only a spectator of the work of art but to join in the performance" (§ 212). Through a contemplative encounter, divine love is made manifest through paint, space, the human body, and sound itself. This love is not an abstraction but worth beholding, wooing us toward a deeper participation in divine life.

The Pastoral Consequences of Slow Catechesis

There are three consequences of a slow, festive catechesis as proposed by the *Directory*'s attention to liturgy, popular piety, and beauty.

First, catechesis in the late modern world simply moves too fast. For those who may be encountering the Christian faith for the first time, schlepping through the entirety of Christian doctrine in fourteen weeks for an hour every Monday may be too much to ask. In addition, many of the praxis pedagogies employed in the Church demand an immediate decision. How will your life change now that you have learned about the Incarnation? What will you do with it? These are fine questions — ones that we each must answer — but not before we have first learned to wonder and to contemplate what is before us. The festive pedagogy of the liturgy needs to be better incorporated into catechesis. Participating in a parish procession, celebrating *Las*

Posadas, singing the Liturgy of the Hours in a parish church, and adoring Christ in the Eucharist are not ritual ways to mark the end of an effective lesson. They are already proposing something to the human person. The catechist has a role to invite Christians to learn both the technique or art and meaning of these practices for the sake of fostering deeper participation.

Second, a slow catechesis will retrieve the importance of matter in the act of catechesis. Think about the average catechetical curriculum in the parish as found in a typical textbook. Yes, sometimes there may be a painting. There may be a suggestion for a song. There may even be a certain ritual action that each person may perform. But these are ancillary to the learning objectives for that unit. Our rush to move through the totality of Christian doctrine means that we ignore the festive dimensions of Christian life including the rich history of Christian art, music, the sacramental rites of the Church, and popular piety. We forget why rose petals matter just as much as books on Christian doctrine.

Third, as the *Directory* hints at, maybe school buildings are not the best places for this festive and thereby slow catechesis (§ 221). Sofia Cavalletti's Catechesis of the Good Shepherd is closer to fostering the kind of catechetical milieu where festive formation may unfold. The teacher is not present to explain the signs and symbols of the liturgy or the Sacred Scriptures. Rather, the catechist in the atrium sets up the environment whereby contemplative wonder and reflection may occur. The catechist in this environment is involved themselves in an occasion of loving contemplation, a slow reflection on the mystery of divine love revealed in the atrium. While Catechesis of the Good Shepherd may be intended for three through to twelve-year-old children, the pedagogical wisdom of the approach has implications for adult life. Catechesis should unfold in a festive space, where there is the reading of the Sacred Scriptures, the capacity to pray, and to contemplative the gift of the liturgical-sacramental signs of the Church. The Order of the Christian Initiation for Adults or the RCIA is especially important here, since the Rite presumes that catechesis will take place primarily in liturgies of the Word. Catechesis itself should be festive.

Of course, a slow catechesis will not heal every malaise of the Church today. But it does provide a festive alternative to a social and cultural world defined by acceleration and work. We are made for festive leisure, to adore the living God. A slow catechesis provides a prophetic witness in the world, one that re-proposes to each person the dignity of inefficient love.

Questions for Conversation:

1. In a world governed by acceleration, what makes it hard to do catechesis today in your setting? How might a slow catechesis—as found in liturgy, popular piety, and encounters with beauty—be salutary for this obsession with speed?
2. Name a Christian doctrine or practice that you regularly contemplate. How have you grown—over the course of your lifetime—into a deeper understanding and commitment to that practice?

Recommended Readings:

Sofia Cavalletti. *The Religious Potential of the Child: Experiencing Scripture and Liturgy with Young Children*, 3rd ed. Chicago, IL: Liturgy Training Publications, 2020.

Roberto S. Goizueta. *Christ Our Companion: Towards a Theological Aesthetics of Liberation*. Maryknoll, NY: Orbis Books, 2009.

Timothy P. O'Malley. *Divine Blessing: Liturgical Formation in the R.C.I.A.* Collegeville, MN: Liturgical Press, 2019.

5
Dialogue - Key to an Evangelizing Catechesis
Jane E. Regan

Like many of us, I would imagine, among my first actions when the *Directory for Catechesis* (henceforth, *Directory*) arrived was to flip to the back of the book and look up my favorite words in the index. For me, these included "adult," "media," "catechist formation," "catechetical leadership." And then I looked for my final and all-time favorite word: "conversation," which is not there. But "dialogue" is, so I followed that, which led me to the topic of this essay.

The opening chapter of the *Directory* concludes with the following heading: "Catechesis as a 'laboratory' of dialogue" (§§ 53-54). I am intrigued. The 1997 *General Directory of Catechesis* (GDC) places the term "dialogue" in its index in reference to "ecumenical" and "interreligious" conversations. This 2020 *Directory* includes these yet offers a broader context for understanding the place of dialogue in catechesis.

Once we have examined the document's use of the term, I propose a description of dialogue that makes more specific the nature and expression of dialogue in the life of the parish and diocese. This is followed by a discussion of the centrality of dialogue to catechesis and its benefits for the individual and the community. The essay concludes with some implications of integrating experience of dialogue in various expressions of catechesis, particularly when working with adults.

Laboratory of Dialogue

At the heart of dialogue in the context of catechesis is the recognition that revelation is the "wonderful *dialogue of salvation*" (§ 53). The story of salvation originates with the divine invitation to human beings to be in relationship with God. The story of salvation from Genesis through today is shaped by the holy rhythm of God continually reaching out to us in love. In all cases, it is God who takes the initiative of inviting us into ever deepening relationships. And we respond in our lives of faith that mature and deepen as we continue to hear God's invitation. It is indeed a "'laboratory' of dialogue."

A survey of the entire *Directory* gives indication of four ways in which the term dialogue is used: as an attitude, as an activity of catechesis, as essential for young adult and adult faith, and as a mode for engaging with the world.

Attitude of Evangelizing Catechesis

As an important moment of evangelization, catechesis shares in the perspectives and approaches that permeate the essential work of evangelization. Describing the general characteristics of the process of evangelization, the *Directory* speaks of drawing "near to all humanity with attitudes of solidarity, fellowship and dialogue, thus bearing witness to the Christians' newness of life" (§ 31). So first, dialogue is seen as a key capacity of those who engage in catechesis, and it underpins the fundamental approach to how we do catechesis.

Component of Catechetical Methodology

We begin examining methodology by considering what the *Directory* refers to as the "divine pedagogy," which is expressed in the ways God has communicated with human beings across history, particularly in the person of Jesus. The Emmaus Road story is a quintessential example of that divine pedagogy: Jesus engaged in dialogue with the two disciples about their experience, their hopes and fears, and their understanding of the tradition; this dialogue concluded with the revelation of the risen Christ and the response of the disciples to go and spread the good news to others. "Catechesis is inspired by this divine pedagogy." As such, it is "a pedagogical action at the service of the dialogue of salvation between God and humanity" (§ 165).

A reading of the *Directory* makes clear that catechesis is a complex and multifaceted reality. "A dynamic and complex reality at the service of the Word of God, it is accompaniment, education, and formation in the faith and for the faith..." (§ 55). Because of its complexity, a variety of activities is employed. For example, when writing about the role of memorization the authors of the *Directory* point out that memorization needs to be used in context with "the other elements of the catechetical process, like relationship, dialogue, reflection, silence and accompaniment" (§ 203). These elements are attitudes or perspectives as well as possible activities within a catechetical encounter.

Essential with Adults

In its discussion of young adults, adults, and the elderly, the *Directory* incorporates the importance of dialogue as both an attitude and an activity. In talking about young adults, the document states: "The Church, manifesting the same solicitude as Jesus, wants to listen to the young people with patience, understand their anxieties, have a true heart-to-heart dialogue, accompany them in discerning their life plan" (§ 251). With young adults, as with all adults, attention to the experiences that they bring to their faith and to catechesis is an essential component and requires that the catechist "establishes a relationship of reciprocity and dialogue in listening to what the Holy Spirit is already silently accomplishing" (§ 197).

In addition, dialogue is an important dimension of the catechesis of adults because of the core tasks that such catechesis hopes to accomplish. It is the adult community that has the primary responsibility for living out and proclaiming the gospel in a way that invites others to engage with the faith. All adults have the responsibility to serve as evangelizing agents, and catechesis must prepare them for this task. The *Directory* states that one of the tasks of adult catechesis is "promoting the formation of mature Christian consciences capable of living the reason for their hope and ready for a serene and intelligent dialogue with contemporary culture" (§ 261). In order to engage in that dialogue with culture, adults need to have active experiences of dialogue within the faith community. The capacity of adults to live out the faith and to give a reason for their hope is enhanced by talking about their faith with other believers. Being comfortable talking about one's faith and listening to the faith stories of others within the parish or pastoral setting is the foundation for being able to talk with others.

Model for Engaging the World
The final context in which dialogue is used is as the mode by which we engage with the world around us. Here I am grouping the document's discussion of

the way we interact with culture, with other religious traditions, and with other Christian denominations. In each case, the attitude and capacity for both listening and dialogue are seen as central. The term "engagement" is used in all of these settings, which is marked by openness to the other. This is discussed in more detail in other chapters within this collection.

So, dialogue within the *Directory* can be examined within the four headings named here: dialogue is an attitude of catechesis, a methodology within catechesis, essential to the catechesis of adults, and reflective of our relationship with the world. Since catechesis is an expression of and participation in the "dialogue of salvation," the writers of the document assert that "the Church desires that catechesis as well should accentuate this dialogical style" (§ 54),

Fostering Dialogue In and For the Church Today
One of the key strengths of the *Directory*'s discussion of dialogue within catechesis is that it does not look at technique but at attitude, perspective, and general approaches. It is a disposition of dialogue that serves

as foundation for our interaction with others and for our living into the mission of evangelization. Since this document addresses the worldwide church, it is appropriate that it speak of general approaches; this allows the national and local churches to incorporate the ideas in a way that is suitable for their context. What are the implications of this call for dialogue as we work to embody the essence of the *Directory* within the U.S. context? How are we going to characterize dialogue in a way that is true to the *Directory* and at the same time appropriate for the U.S. church?

Before proposing a working definition of dialogue, it is helpful to articulate the contribution that engaging in dialogue makes to the person of faith and to the community. While the mode of dialogue—writing, reflection, or small group conversation, for example—may vary, within the context of catechesis it is always in service to shaping ever more effective agents of evangelization. The church "exists in order to evangelize" (*Evangelii Nuntiandi*, §14); and catechesis must prepare us for that task.

Formative role of Dialogue

At a fundamental level, engaging in dialogue gives us the occasion to both speak and hear ourselves speak about what we believe and understand about our faith. For many adults in our faith communities, there are few opportunities to speak about their faith with other adults. Structures that support dialogue provide the opening for people to articulate their faith, to place it outside of themselves, as it were. This gives believers the possibility to critically examine aspects of their beliefs, for both meaning and implications, thus deepening their faith. At the same time, dialogue allows us to hear the faith expressions of others. Realizing that differing ways of understanding and practicing the faith exist within the parish community provides all with other lenses for viewing church teachings and traditions. Opportunities for dialogue have the potential to lead to a renewed and deeper understanding and appreciation of our faith.

Forming a Dialogical Church

Dialogue is formative of the community of faith as well. Dialogue as both attitude and methodology contribute to the formation of a dialogical church. At our best, dialogue is not simply something we do; it is how we enter into everything we do. A dialogical church is marked by an emphasis on relationality, a spirit of openness, a stance of careful listening. This is a point highlighted by Daniella Zsupan-Jerome, in her chapter in this collection, as she addresses the important orientation and skills of listening and participation. And it is through engaging in dialogue that we gain the necessary skills as individuals and as a community; we learn how to enter into dialogue by doing it. It is important to recognize that we can only effectively have the hard conversations—about race, or immigration, or authority (ecclesial and civic)—if we learn how to have effective dialogue in the less contentious aspects of our lives together while on committees, advisory boards, or pastoral councils.

One of the characteristics that marks the ecclesiology of Pope Francis is synodality. The *Directory* quotes the Pope: "A synodal Church is a Church which listens, which realizes that listening 'is more than simply hearing'. It is a mutual listening in which everyone has something to learn. The faithful people, the college of bishops, the Bishop of Rome: all listening to each other, and all listening to the Holy Spirit" (§ 289). Again, catechesis must prepare us for being a synodal church.

Dialogue: A Working Definition

As we think about how to put dialogue into practice in all the settings where adults learn to live their faith, having a clear definition of what dialogue looks like in practice is helpful. In my own work, I have tended to use the word conversation rather than dialogue. But, from my read of the *Directory*, I believe that my description of conversation from *Where Two or Three Are Gathered* is also a way to delineate dialogue as it is used here. Conversation or dialogue can be described as "the sustained, engaged, and critical interchange between two or more people constituted by active listening and respectful speaking around issues that matter" (98).

The focus of dialogue is on issues that matter to us, to the church, and to the world. This isn't simply pleasant chit-chat or idle discussion; dialogue engages us in life questions: How should we spend our time and money? How should we raise our children? How should we decide whom we vote for in an election? On a community level, some of the same questions apply: How do we spend parish money and how are budgeting decisions made? What does it mean for a parish to live out the preferential option for the poor? How do we—as individuals and as a faith community—be intentionally and actively anti-racist? Ultimately, issues that matter are faith issues. Providing opportunities to engage in conversation about these issues and many others is central to the work of forming adult faith.

In terms that are similar to those in the *Directory*, this definition pairs dialogue with openness, listening, and respect. It also describes the interchanges of dialogue as "sustained, engaged, and critical." It is *sustained* in that it happens for an extended block of time over a sufficient period of time. It is *engaged* to the degree that in the give-and-take of genuine dialogue, everyone involved invests themselves fully in the process; the participants are willing to suspend judgement to listen and to hear the other. And dialogue is *critical* when there is an openness to questioning taken-for-granted perspectives, approaches, and presumptions about how things work; critical dialogue invites us to ask why we think or act the way we do and how else we might frame the topic.

Dialogue, as framed by the writers of the *Directory*, is both an attitude and a methodology; it is central to adult catechesis and is key to our effective engagement with the world. Its importance for catechesis is its faith formative impact. Through engaging in dialogue, our understanding of our own faith and the faith and beliefs of others is enhanced; our capacity and skills for dialogue are strengthened; and, we become people who see dialogue as essential to being and becoming an ever more effective evangelizing church.

Three Caveats

While I think the presence and explication of dialogue within the *Directory* is an important contribution to our understanding of catechesis, there are three concerns that warrant exploration. First, having it in the document does not make it happen. We need to remember that this is in the form of an aspiration rather than a present reality. It is essential that we acknowledge that integrating a dialogical style into catechesis, particularly adult catechesis, will require the concerted effort of catechetical leaders at every level.

Second, the writers of the document do not seem to account for the contexts in which dialogue is impossible. Dialogue with racist or homophobic persons or groups may not even begin; dialogue with someone who despises you because of political affiliation or ideological convictions can be threatening; dialogue may be difficult in a culture in which being a woman means that one is without rights. It is important to keep in mind that there are times in which intentional silence or private writing or reflection may be the better option.

Third, in reading through the *Directory*, what appears to be missing is a sense that the church could also learn and change through the process of dialogue. There is a certain focus on the important things that "we" (which I read as church leadership) have to share with "them" in dialogue. And it seems that activities of dialogue can be used more as a lure to get the youth or adult engaged than as a genuine exchange with another with an openness to change (e.g. § 29, § 252).

Implications to Consider

But, what can this look like in our local church or parish? What are the effects of this for the work of the catechetical leader at the parish or diocesan level? I propose three implications for your consideration. Perhaps you can think of them as invitations to think and think again about your role and about the complex work of catechesis. Perhaps you could enter into dialogue with your colleagues about these ideas.

First, emphasizing its dialogical nature invites us to see catechesis in a broader context. As Susanna Singer argues in her chapter in this collection, catechesis—particularly adult catechesis—goes beyond programming. While incorporating dialogue into our Lenten program or sacramental formation for parents is important, we recognize that the opportunities for adults to be in dialogue extends far beyond the activities labeled catechesis.

Committee meetings, advisory boards, and working groups of catechists, are all potentially contexts where topics that matter are discussed, the skills of dialogue can be learned, and faith is formed. Moving beyond the busy agendas to allow time and space for dialogue both about the topic at hand and about the implications for one's faith is an important step.

The second implication flows from the first: continuing to break down the silos that separate aspects of parish life from one another. Being a dialogical faith community both presumes and enhances the interaction and dialogue across the various dimensions of parish life. Just as a dialogical community calls for dialogue across differing committees and boards, it also invites dialogue between different theological or political ideologies. How can catechesis be the context for preparing people for other expressions of dialogue within and outside the faith community?

The third implication centers on these questions: Who is not present in the dialogue? Whose voices are not heard? At a basic level, this is asking about who within the parish is not well represented on committee or boards or in the ranks of the catechists or the liturgical ministers. At a next step, is the question of who is marginalized or silenced by the teachings or tenor of the parish? On the one hand this could include members of the LGBTQ+ community or immigrant groups; on the other it could include those whose theological beliefs or practices are out of keeping with the norm of the parish. This is an ongoing issue in most parishes and the resolution begins by asking the critical questions named earlier: Who is not present in the dialogue? Whose voices are not heard?

The *Directory* proposes that catechesis is a "laboratory of dialogue" as it should reflect the dialogical style of the pedagogy of God, the One who is always inviting us into relationship. Bringing that to life in the U.S. Catholic Church has the potential to enhance the faith and strengthen the evangelizing capacity particularly among adults.

Questions for Conversation:
1 How is dialogue, as described in the *Directory* and developed in this chapter, an important aspect of

your own thinking about catechesis? What forms does dialogue take in your setting? How might that be enhanced? What do you see as the primary challenges to making dialogue a central aspect of the catechetical endeavor?
2. I have named three implications for how we think about our work. Discuss any that are significant for you? What others come to mind in your pastoral setting?

Recommended Reading

William Issacs. *Dialogue: The Art of Thinking Together*. New York, NY: Doubleday, 1999.

Jane E. Regan. *Toward an Adult Church: A Vision of Faith Formation*. Chicago, IL: Loyola Press, 2002.

Jane E. Regan, *Where Two or Three Are Gathered: Transforming the Parish Through Communities of Practice*. New York, NY: Paulist Press, 2016.

6
Enfleshing Catechesis[1] Through Embodied Space
Lakisha R. Lockhart

I am a Black woman.
I have big bold curls that will not be tamed.
I have full lips, a button nose, and high cheekbones.
My eyes are rather small, and often look like I am squinting when I smile.
I have curvy hips that make very lean and narrow chairs uncomfortable.
I am 5'2" and often stand on my tippy toes to reach things.
I am a mother, wife, religious educator and practical theologian with a doctorate.
I have been abused, objectified, belittled and I hold privilege.
I use movement, and play to teach, to learn, to be, and make meaning in the world.
I am a Black woman in a Black woman body.

---

1 The title of this chapter is inspired by M. Shawn Copeland's book *Enfleshing Freedom: Body, Race, and Being* (Minneapolis, MN: Fortress Press, 2010).

See me. Allow my narrative to take up space and help you see me as more than just my Black woman body. Really *seeing* people and making space for their full-embodied realities is not easy, and yet necessary to enflesh catechesis.

When I read the *Directory for Catechesis* (henceforth, *Directory*) this notion of a "pedagogy of the incarnation" and "plurality of methods" really spoke to me (*Directory*, § 194-195). These two things spoke to me because, while I find them necessary for religious education, I also find them to be lacking in many church spaces and religious education curriculum. Many spaces and curriculum are disembodied, lacking connection from their given community and context, which often causes more harm and hurt than healing. When catechesis is not done with actual flesh and bodies in mind and involved, everyone suffers.

The truth is that no matter what, I am and always will be what you read in the beginning—a Black woman in a Black woman body. The way in which I view, move in the world and take up space is both enhanced and affected by my lived reality, and experience in a Black woman's body—my embodied reality. Being in this body I have been in places that were not healthy or "safe," and were in fact quite harmful. Being in this body, I have heard and seen things that did not affirm my existence, often from within the very church that also professed me to be a beloved and cherished child of God. However, when all the images around were of a white, blond haired and blue eyed Jesus and God, I did not see myself reflected or affirmed. When I was told "God wants you to be pure for Him. To be white as snow, not black and dirty," I saw my skin color as bad and my gender as less important than "Him." This disembodied understanding and usage of colonized language and notion of body that happened in religious and church spaces and environments that were supposed to build me up, shape me, and help me feel valued would take years to unlearn and decenter.

I have mentioned just a few of my encounters, of which there are many. If we include those of our siblings of other races, ethnicities, gender identities, sexual orientations, and abilities, just to name a few, I am sure this could go on for pages. Herein lies the heart of both my concern and hope in this chapter. Many religious institutions and churches claim an incarnational catechesis or pedagogy in which the word is made flesh, but the very bodies that are present are not welcome, heard, represented or seen as bodies with honor and dignity made in *imago dei*. How can we make the word flesh while daily denying the flesh of others in words and actions? How can we truly begin to enflesh catechesis? I believe that in order for catechesis to be incarnational, there must be a space or environment (I will use the two interchangeably) in which all persons cannot only be seen, but also see and feel themselves reflected. This does not mean "safe"—which I will expand on later. However, it does mean that a space is created in which questions can be asked, all people are seen as whole and loveable as they are, inclusive language is spoken, actions and images reflect those present and beyond, and people can have real and honest dialogue that holds everyone accountable to live out the justice of God in the world. While enfleshing catechesis demands many things, for the sake of this chapter, I will focus on two: 1. cultivating space for all bodies; and 2. decolonizing language and bodies within that space. Once we engage in this work and begin to cultivate this kind of environment, we can not only teach and preach an enfleshed catechesis that is incarnational, but we can all live out the word in and through our glorious flesh.

Cultivating Space for All Bodies

"We must create safe spaces for our members." I often hear this when discussing matters of embodied learning and creating religious spaces, especially for young adults. We want to create environments that are "welcoming and well-kept, that they convey a climate of familiarity that fosters serene involvement in community activities" (§ 222). However, I would like to push back and challenge this notion. As someone who has had the privilege of working with many Black and Brown youth, I had an amazing conversation with a young Black man once. We were talking about cultivating space together and he said something to the effect of, "safe space is bullshit. I am a Black man living in this country and I ain't never safe. So, don't promise me something you can't deliver." Let that sit with you for a moment. "Safe space is bullshit. I am a Black man living in this country and I ain't never safe. So, don't promise me something you can't deliver."

I have kept these words in my heart when I do youth ministry, when I teach, as I raise my Black son, as I write, and as I live out my own faith. As a result, I have come to have several commitments and new understandings about the cultivation of shared embodied space. My first understanding is that to be able to even name a space or use the word "safe" is a privilege that many will never know or experience. Therefore, if everyone cannot feel "safe," then no one should feel safe. We should all be in a space where we can name and wrestle with the tension and discomfort that may arise. Some would name this a "brave" space, where people can choose to be brave and courageous by realizing and naming places of privilege, difference, and similarities, holding each other accountable in love and creating community in spite of. Some have let the given community and context name their space for themselves and let them decide what they would like their space to be and to do. For me, I choose to create "clearing spaces." This is a term that novelist, editor, and professor Toni Morrison has written about in many of her books, *Beloved* in particular. A clearing space is a space where people can come and dance, laugh, play, call each other in and out, let their hair down, a space of possibility and grace, and most importantly, a space to be unapologetic and free—a womanist space. For me, this is the kind of space in which teaching and learning can thrive for all bodies.

The second understanding that I gained from this brilliant young black man was that I should never promise something that I cannot deliver. I actually cannot guarantee any one's safety. I cannot promise that someone else will not say or do something offensive that destroys trust and leaves someone feeling belittled or devalued. To try to do so is counterproductive, dangerous and practically sets up the environment to fail as we are all human and will in fact mess up. However, if we promise a space that will be courageous, that will name and wrestle with tension, that will call out acts of violence and hold each other accountable to be and do better, then that is something that I believe people can understand and grow into. Is this not what our authentic human existence demands? A space where we can be human and exist in a way that feels real and authentic to who we are? If in fact, as the *Directory* states, every "culture, society, and community...expresses and communicates itself through space" we must do our best to tend to that reality (§§ 194, 221).

In tending to that reality, we must be honest with ourselves and ask the necessary questions when naming and creating space. In thinking about the importance of space, I cannot help but think of Theresa O'Keefe's chapter in this collection as she looks at research about the number of young people who are or have become disaffiliated with the church. I wonder, if the right kind of space was made for them, would they have stayed and felt more of a sense of belonging? Take a moment to visualize your space. Who is present and who is not? Is your space accessible to those differently abled? Are the images, languages, leaders and practices welcoming and affirming to our LGBTQ+ siblings? To our racially and ethnically diverse siblings? To our siblings of various ages and economic situations? Are those not present not welcome or not there by choice, circumstance or design and why? When curating space it is crucial to make a space in which all bodies are valued and seen as made in *imago dei*.

Enfleshing Demands Decolonizing

The second demand of enfleshing catechesis is decolonizing language and bodies within and around the cultivated space. The *Directory* states it well by saying "the spaces for catechesis are settings in which the community expresses its own way of evangelizing. In the current social and cultural context, it is appropriate to reflect on the specificity of the places of catechesis as instruments of proclamation and of education to human relationships" (§ 222). This is absolutely true and necessary to understand in the cultivating of embodied space for community. Cultivating the right kind of space for our community and context will take time, energy, intentionality, specificity and a great deal of trial and error. We will not always get it right, but it is in the process of adjusting and trying that we learn and get better. In order to do this we must decolonize our language and notion of bodies. While these two may seem like separate things they are intricately linked as one cannot be discussed without affecting the other. Our perception and history with language has affected our attitudes and behaviors with bodies, specifically with non-white bodies and we must name that, interrogate it and begin to decolonize both in order to make space for the embodied realities—the physical bodies and lived experiences—of all people.

"Language, with its relational meanings, is an essential part of human experience. Catechesis is calibrated according to the diversity of persons, of their culture, history, or environment, of their way of and capacity for understanding reality" (§ 204). Language is indeed an essential part of human existence and necessary for understanding persons and their experiences and realities within their physical bodies. In order to discuss why decolonization is necessary, we must understand, as mentioned above, the colonized history of language and embodied expression. While I will not cover the entire history in this short chapter, I do want to offer a few important highlights. As white, western, male, heteronormative, Christian culture was the dominant culture of much of the history of the U.S., all other cultures were seen as less than and inferior. This includes language and bodily expression. Many enslaved and non-white persons were physically taken from places where they already possessed languages, cultures, and communication and expression systems of their own. However, when they were brought to this country as enslaved persons their cultures, languages, and even physical bodies were colonized. Their indigenous languages and means of communication were not valued, their very identities and places in society were forced upon them by those in power. There were actually laws that disallowed and criminalized reading and education of formal English for most enslaved and non-white people. The enslaved would be whipped and beaten for attempting to learn or communicate. Their physical bodies were no longer there own as they became subject to harsh labor, abuse, rape, and were bought and sold like cattle. In colonizing language, cultural bodily expression in all its forms (music, art, dance, laughter, cooking, etc.) was colonized too. It was clear that these other epistemological, ontological, and embodied ways of being were dismissed as groups of people were forced to conform to a certain way of life.

The colonizing dominance of Christianity played a major role in this cultural formation, social construction and living out of what Emilie Townes calls, in her book *Womanist Ethics and the Cultural Production of Evil*, the "fantastic hegemonic imagination." Specific passages and translations of what was considered to be Sacred Scripture were used to keep enslaved persons docile and frightened and some passages were not allowed to be read at all. Willie James Jennings, in his book *The Christian Imagination*, notes, "the intimacy that marks Christian history is a painful one, one in which the joining often meant oppression, violence, and death, if not of bodies then most certainly of ways of life, forms of language, and visions of the world" (p. 6). This molding, framing, and subjugating of the word of God to the system of chattel slavery, according to Jennings, explains why "Christianity in the Western world lives and moves within a diseased social imagination" (p. 8).

Sadly, the Bible and Christianity are still being misused for the gain of those in power today. This understanding of the impact of history among persons as well as religious institutions is vital when teaching and learning about religious traditions and living out one's faith. It is those in power who have resisted diversity and difference and prostituted Christianity for their own personal gain. In his chapter in this collection, Steffano Montano mentions the need to not only engage in more truth-telling, as I have done here, but to also do the hard anti-racism work required to really see and understand this history and how its effects have rippled throughout time. There are a multitude of ways in which to live and have being, and a God of love, justice, freedom and reconciliation values all of us. This is why decolonizing language, bodily expression and communication, in all forms (i.e. storytelling, art, music, dance, digital technology, and poetry, etc.) in our spaces and valuing not only ways of knowing and being, but the very bodies which hold all this history and knowledge is crucial (§ 207-221).

Toward an Authentically Enfleshed Catechesis
Cultivating an environment is like learning to dance. First, we must feel out our space, decide what dance we are going to do and then learn its history and the steps involved so that we can dance with understanding, confidence, and passion. Much like how we must learn and understand the history of language and body and their historical implications so we can understand the need to decolonize them. Once there is an understanding, appreciation and knowledge of the basics, we can begin to add a partner. This is a very scary and vulnerable step, as bodies must connect. When adding a partner there must be consideration of the partner's body, movement, vulnerability and understanding of the dance as we find our new rhythm together. This is exactly what happens when we cultivate space with others, we must take their bodies, understandings,

vulnerabilities and very personhood into consideration and adjust as needed until we can all find a new rhythm where everyone can learn, share, and be vulnerable together.

This means that first, and foremost we must look at ourselves. Where are the places that we are using colonized language and forms of communication and why? What art is on our walls and why? I would recommend we take a walk around our church or area with new eyes that might belong to someone who is the exact opposite of us. Look at the space including every piece of art, every bulletin board, every pew, every stair, every doorway...everything. What does it communicate and in what language? Do we physically feel welcome and represented? Note where things can be adjusted, changed, taken down, removed, highlighted more, and added. Then invite someone else to do the same. Listen, discuss, and then adjust.

Once we look at ourselves we must get to know the people in our community and context. We can use my introduction as a rough example and invite the people in our community and context to name who they are, what they experience in their bodies, how they navigate through the world and where they see the divine. I have done words here, but in hopes of decolonizing this exercise, open this up to be expressed in any way desired. It can be a poem, a rap song, a dance, a screenplay, a painting, a Lego tower, etc. The important part is to create an embodied space where all can name themselves for themselves in a language that feels like "home" to them, not us. Listen, discuss, and then adjust.

We often know and value various epistemologies and ontological realities and I would like to be sure we include physical bodily realities. How people come to know, teach, learn and have their very being is affected by their physical and bodily existence—much like what I expressed in the beginning of this chapter. My world is shaped not just because I am a scholar and a mother, but because I am and will always be a scholar and a mother in a black woman body. My embodied reality is an epistemology and ontological reality in itself. It is my way of being and knowing and we must cultivate spaces in which this kind of embodied knowing and learning are valued, practiced and seen as important for all bodies. Decolonizing language and bodies are beginning steps in cultivating an embodied space in which we can not only teach, learn and preach a catechesis that is incarnational, but we can all live out the word, in whatever medium and expression feels right for us, in and through our bodies.

Questions for Conversation:
1 In what ways are your curriculum, practices, sermons, bible studies, and rituals colonized? What is the impact on your community and context? What one thing can you do today to create the kind of embodied space, which allows for the enfleshing of catechesis for all in your community and context?
2 Whose bodies are considered important and not important in your community and context and why? Whose bodies are seen and unseen in your community and context and why? Whose bodies are depicted, displayed on walls and referenced and whose are not in your community and context and why?

Recommended Readings:

M. Shawn Copeland. *Enfleshing Freedom: Body, Race, and Being*. Minneapolis, MN: Fortress Press, 2010.

Willie James Jennings. *The Christian Imagination: Theology and the Origins of Race*. New Haven, CT: Yale University Press, 2010.

Emilie Maureen Townes. *Womanist Ethics and the Cultural Production of Evil*. New York, NY: Palgrave Macmillian, 2006.

Contexts

7
Antiracism and the 2020 Directory for Catechesis
Steffano Montano

As 2020 has revealed, racism remains a persistent social sin in the United States of America. From the unjustifiable police shootings of people of color, to the outsize effect of COVID-19 on Black and Brown communities, race remains an important source of data that reveals some of the inequalities and injustices that our society metes out as a consequence of keeping people of color from positions of decision-making power. Antiracism recognizes that racism is a given condition of the status quo and that a neutral stance towards racism ultimately perpetuates that same status quo. It is therefore a call to stand actively and openly against racism and a commitment to live out that call on a daily basis. It is also a commitment that the United States Conference of Catholic Bishops (USCCB) has engaged through the creation of an Ad Hoc Committee Against Racism and the writing of a pastoral letter on antiracism in 2018, *Open Wide Our*

Hearts: The Enduring Call to Love. Yet a look at the divide on issues of racial justice among Catholics in the U.S. shows that many do not believe that their faith calls them to antiracism. Indeed, in December of 2020 one of the largest Catholic radio stations in the country dropped its one program hosted by and geared towards Black Catholics, *Morning Glory*, because a growing number of the station's supporters complained that Gloria Purvis, the show's host, was too vocal in her denunciation of systematic racism.

This has not always been the case. While it is true that some Catholic priests, bishops, laity, and organizations did perpetuate racism as part of the colonial structure, did buy enslaved persons, and helped to promote segregation post-emancipation, it is also true that many Catholic priests, sisters, and laity were on the front lines of the civil rights movement. Too many Catholics in the United States today are disconnected from this tradition, and from the theological anthropology that guides it. It seems as if the only Catholics who are concerned are the ones whom racism and white supremacy impacts the most directly: Black, Asian, Indigenous, and Latinx Catholics, as well as those who fight for gender and sexual equality and their allies. It is clear that we can contribute to "righting the ship" however, if we can include this tradition, this anthropology, and these practices within our regular catechetical efforts. Doing so can reconnect the lived faith and practices of Catholics with the stated beliefs the church puts out. How might we reorient the formation of Catholics towards anti-racism? Does the new 2020 *Directory for Catechesis* (henceforth, *Directory*) provide room for us to do so?

Catechesis in Particular Churches

The particular Churches, in all their expressions, carry out the task of proclaiming the Gospel in the different contexts in which they are rooted... Different geographical contexts, settings of a religious nature, cultural tendencies – although they do not directly concern ecclesial catechesis – shape the inner physiognomy of our contemporaries, at whose service the Church places herself, and so they cannot help but be an object of discernment in view of the catechetical initiative (*Directory*, § 9).

An important recommendation arising from the *Directory* is that we must pay attention to our context, and specifically to how our context has formed the inner workings of our sisters and brothers. If we are to take this call from the *Directory* seriously, the particular church of the United States must engage with the tools and practices of anti-racism precisely because the gospel's light, the good news of Christ, must be brought to bear on the injustices suffered by so many of our church's members.

Discussing racism amongst people of faith is a tricky subject. Many believe that we entered a post-racial society. As proof, they point to events, such as when the Civil Rights legislation was passed in the 1960s, when people of color broke through into some leadership and wealth in the latter half of the 20th century, again when Barack Obama was elected president in 2008 and 2012, and again in 2021 when Kamala Harris became the first woman of color (and multiple ethnicities) elected vice president. Yet the reality of the systemic suffering of people of color is irrefutable and easily documented across the sectors of public health, incarceration, and housing, to name a few. It is to these realities that the church must proclaim, in word and deed, that Black Lives Matter, that Brown Lives Matter, that Indigenous Lives Matter, precisely because they seem to matter less to the justice systems of the United States. Yet the phrase itself has taken on a considerable political weight, and many within positions of power in Catholic circles have chosen to reject the phrase out of a theology of salvation that seeks to remove distinctions between peoples in favor of a universal identity under Christ. "All Lives Matter" is their retort to the message, often juxtaposed with the image of Christ dying on the cross. The theological statement behind such an image supports a theology of salvation that ignores Christ's preferential option for the poor in his own ministry. Even among those that believe that racism exists as a problem at some level, the prevalent theory of change is that belief in Christ and "loving one's neighbor as one's self" is enough to undo racism in our society. Is ignoring racism in catechesis, an effective theory of change for combating racism in the United States?

Research from practical theologians and educational theorists, among others, proves that ignoring the reality of racism has no effect in overturning its suffering – indeed the opposite is often true. As Montague Williams shows in his book *Church in Color: Youth Ministry, Race, and the Theology of Martin Luther King, Jr.*, children and teens, for example, notice the silence of churches on racism, leading them to believe that church spaces are inappropriate for discussing how racism affects their lives and the lives of their friends and loved ones:

> Post-racial youth ministry [and catechesis] requires young people to adjust to a discipleship that ultimately declare that their bodies do not matter in the life worth living. They are offered a portrayal of Christian living that embraces color-blindness and welcomes standards and imagination that derive from racialized hierarchy to be normative and virtuous (p. 58).

This phenomenon furthers the disconnect between lived faith and the struggle against racism. If catechesis ignores the realities of racism in the U.S., it shades the Gospel's light of goodness and truth for their lives and furthers the infection of racism among our white sisters and brothers trying to deepen their understanding of their faith. It also ignores the history of Christian support of and resistance to racism in the United States. In order to take our U.S. cultural context seriously in the ministry of catechesis, we must begin by telling the *truth* about our context, including our church's relationship to racism.

Truth-Telling

Truth-telling does not only proclaim, uphold, and protect the diversity of each of our beings, but also points to the sin that we are each culpable in, personally and socially. Truth-telling for antiracism does not shy away from the ways that Catholics across North America, from colonial times to the present, have both supported and stood against racism, slavery, segregation, and newer forms of discrimination. Truth-telling encourages each of us to tell the stories of ourselves, our families, and our people in these histories, and to seek forgiveness and justice in each of these areas. Truth-telling encourages a care-full listening within catechetical spaces, as each of the students are asked to dive into their own family and personal histories regarding their racial, cultural, and ethnic identities (among others). These histories reveal the ways that we have been impacted by systemic racism, and in telling these truths we come to better understand how these systems operate and how they are handed down across generations. In telling these truths, we also uncover the many traditions of resistance to racism, and the heroes these traditions inspired. Doing so answers the invitation the *Directory* issues "to engage with the complexity of the contemporary world, in which very different elements are blended together" (§ 9). Indeed, the *Directory* states:

> Catechesis is placed at the service of the believer's response of faith, enabling [them] to live the Christian life in a state of conversion. This is in

essence a matter of fostering the internalization of the Christian message, through the catechetical dynamism which in its progression knows how to integrate listening, discernment, and purification. Such catechetical action is not limited to the individual believer, but is addressed to the whole Christian community in order to support the missionary commitment of evangelization. Catechesis also encourages the incorporation of individuals and of the community into the social cultural context, assisting the Christian interpretation of history and fostering the social commitment of Christians (§ 73).

In order to avoid the harm to people of color that Williams' research reveals, religion and racial justice are not to be divorced. History shows us that some of the most prominent leaders for racial justice were also religious figures. The Rev. Dr. Martin Luther King, Jr. led the most successful movement to combat racism in the history of the United States, not regardless of his religious convictions, but precisely because of them. His work organizing people of color and their allies in marches and other acts of non-violent civil disobedience was thoroughly grounded in his faith.

There are many similar examples in the Catholic world such as Antonio de Montesinos, Bartolomé de las Casas, Katherine Drexel, Peter Claver, Augustus Tolton, and Thea Bowman. They are notable within our tradition and serve as important examples of Catholics who have stood prominently against racism. Along with the histories of resistance these figures embody coexist the histories of many others who supported racist policies. Indeed, every one of these anti-racist religious leaders were struggling against a status quo that was both secular and ecclesial. The first step in reorienting our catechetical efforts towards anti-racism is acknowledging these histories. They are what German Catholic theologian Johan Baptist Metz calls "dangerous memories," and they serve not only to help Catholics today understand our past, but to guide them into an identity that stands up to racism and other systemic evils. Doing so would help move catechesis beyond being a mere guide to beliefs, as

Thomas Groome asserts in his chapter in this collection, and closer to a formative, holistic framework that encourages encounter between personal practices, history, culture, and Christ. It also sets a grounding of hope for Catholics of color, who continue to see a church that rejects their struggles for justice.

Truth-telling about the present moment is another important aspect of this commitment. It is important for the faith and moral development of those involved in our catechetical ministries to tell the truth about the ways that Black and Brown people, including Black and Brown Catholics, are struggling in the U.S. in 2021. It is important to highlight the stories of struggle, resistance, and resilience from Black and Brown Catholics, especially when those stories highlight how their faith helped them to survive, resist, and reimagine themselves as Catholics. These stories serve as a resource for all Catholics and have been left untapped for too long by catechetical leaders and resource developers. These stories can equip Catholics of all races and ethnicities not only to resist systemic sins in their own lives, but to practice their faith creatively, to breathe new life into them, and to regenerate how it is that the coming generations understand faith and hope amidst a secularized milieu.

In the area of racism, some of our religious organizations have begun this process of reckoning as well. Georgetown University recently admitted its involvement in selling enslaved men and women in order to help finance the school. The school decided to not only admit to this history, but, as the *Directory* calls (§ 73), to also model a way forward to healing and to a lived conversion by extending reparations to the descendants of the people they bought and sold. The Catholic Sisters of the Society of the Sacred Heart have done similarly, creating a reparations fund to help finance educational scholarships for Black people after recounting their history of owning 150 Black persons in the 1800s. These examples model a way forward in courage, humility, justice, and reconciliation as particular churches continue to discern, as the *Directory* also calls (§ 9), how to purify themselves of the sin of racism.

Building for Belonging

Within catechetical spaces, a commitment to anti-racist work requires not only using the tools of anti-bias curriculum experts, such as the implicit associations test, the identity wheel, and other resources. It also demands creating spaces where students are asked to explore their own biases are and name where they come from, and discover how they affect themselves and others. This is an essential part of truth-telling about ourselves oriented towards "listening, discernment, and purification" (§ 73). This work is uncomfortable, and often comes with push-back from those afflicted by white fragility, but it can be ingrained in the examination of conscience we ask all of our faithful to practice. Helpful in this work is cultivating ways of being church for lament and grace, as Nathaniel Samuels puts forward in his chapter in this collection. A commitment to antiracism in our catechesis should recognize that teaching against racism requires reorienting our traditional canons of educational materials to include the voices, experiences, and theological contributions of Black and Brown Catholics. Likewise, the curricula and materials that are created for catechesis should be built not only for teaching anti-bias, but to reflect an epistemology, pedagogy, and faith experience that is more inclusive of non-white races and non-European ethnicities. Looking beyond the European and U.S. culture pushes back against the history of colonization, and the harms of missionary education to the embodied realities and cultural heritage of our ancestors. Hosffman Ospino's chapter in this collection is an invitation to embrace an intercultural perspective for catechesis.

In her work *Enfleshing Freedom*, M. Shawn Copeland states that the Eucharistic celebration requires that we break down biases that prevent division if we are truly to embody Christ through God's church in the world. Furthermore,

> If my sister or brother is not at the table, we are not the flesh of Christ. If my sister's mark of sexuality must be obscured, if my brother's mark of race must be disguised, if my sister's mark of culture must be repressed, then we are not the flesh of

Christ. For, it is through and in Christ's own flesh that the "other" is my sister, is my brother; indeed, the other is me (*yo soy tu otro yo*). Unless our sisters and brothers are beside and with each of us, we are not the flesh of Christ (p. 82).

Becoming the flesh of Christ, a Eucharistic calling for each of us as well as for the church, is one that we must take seriously. It calls us towards not only an ethical practice, but a way of being that does not deny the divine dignity of humanity within anyone we encounter. Further, it seeks to celebrate the diverse expressions of that dignity present across our genders, races, ethnicities, cultures, sexualities, and abilities. It seeks not to punish others for their existence, but rather to speak truth to the Gospel and proclaim, "yes, this is Christ among us." Indeed, the only bias towards other persons we are called to practice is one that favors the poor and vulnerable (Matthew 25:31-46). Drawing from Paul's letter to the Galatians, we understand that one aspect of our identity as Christians is precisely to refute harmful biases. The *Directory*, while never mentioning racism or racial bias outright, does reiterate in several instances the importance of combating hate and prejudice, especially through encounter, dialogue, and for the sake of building a more inclusive community (§ 270, § 274, § 347, § 361).

Inclusion, especially of diverse cultures, races, and ethnicities, is an aspect that needs greater attention among catechetical efforts. Fortunately, research exists for this to be easily included among catechetical resources and curricula. The work of such scholars as Beverly Daniel Tatum, Derald Wing Sue, Janet Helms, and many others can help catechetical leaders to expand on their commitments to structural developmental psychology to include the important goal of battling toxic forms of racial identity development. The use of culturally sustaining pedagogy within our catechetical spaces would also contribute to antiracist efforts. Growing up Cuban American, for instance, meant that most of my own religious education ignored the many ways that my family practiced our Catholic faith, leaving me in doubt not only of my own family's Catholicity, but also of my ability to understand whether the Cuban American experience had anything distinctive or worthwhile to say about our faith.

Towards An Antiracist Catechesis

An antiracist catechesis inspires our church to commit to being a more just and equitable place for all by challenging our society's brokenness and pushing for a place where all can truly belong. It has the power to generate both "new works of mercy that respond to the needs of the present" and enter into a dialogue that is a "valuable contribution to peace" (§ 52, § 53). An antiracist catechesis does what the *Directory* advises by focusing on what is necessary in our particular context and on an internalization of the Christian message that allows for life in a state of conversion.

It equips our faithful to do this by helping them to know and speak the truth about race. Doing this requires catechists to intentionally include the history of slavery, segregation, and racism that many Catholics engaged in, alongside the history of resistance, resilience, reparation, and reconciliation that we can also claim. An antiracist catechesis also focuses on better understanding the ways that racial, ethnic, and cultural identities have been shaped, and calls for catechists to employ culturally sustaining practices in their ministry and community.

Finally, it gives us an understanding of the ways we view others, and how others should be treated, and to continually check in with that understanding through an examination of conscience as we strive to walk towards the listening, discernment, and purification necessary for the particular church in the United States (§ 9, § 73).

Questions for Conversation:
1. Is racism discussed within your catechetical spaces, either as a current reality or something related to our faith?
2. How are race, ethnicity, and culture diversely included within your catechetical practice? In what ways can you shape this inclusion to help those whom you minister to develop a sense of belonging in the church out of their own racial, ethnic, and cultural identities?

Recommended Readings:

M. Shawn Copeland. *Enfleshing Freedom: Body, Race, and Being*. Minneapolis, MN: Fortress Press, 2009.

Montague Williams. *Church in Color: Youth Ministry, Race, and the Theology of Martin Luther King, Jr.* Waco, TX: Baylor University Press, 2020.

United States Conference of Catholic Bishops. *Open Wide Our Hearts: The Enduring Call to Love – A Pastoral Letter Against Racism.* Washington D.C.: USCCB, 2020.

8
The Horizon and the Guiding Community
Theresa A. O'Keefe

How do we best communicate a vision – an ultimate horizon on life – so that others will commit to it? Since it is ultimate, touching all aspects of life, it would require creativity and diverse forms. It would require the witness of lives guided by the vision. Such is the work of catechesis. Yet, too often people reduce catechesis to the transmission of information, with a focus on dogma and moral teachings. Such a reduction does an injustice to the vision and fails in its objective of bringing others to deep commitment.

When we think of catechesis, especially for those maturing to adulthood, it is important to keep in mind the depth and breadth of what we are communicating, and offer an appropriate response. The 2020 *Directory for Catechesis* (henceforth *Directory*) asserts the foundational goal of catechesis is to make "the initial conversion ripen and helps Christians to give a complete meaning to their existence, educating them in a *mentality of faith*, in keeping with the Gospel, to the point of gradually coming to feel, think and act like Christ" (§ 77). In this chapter, I propose essential considerations for catechizing young people – anyone between their early teens to their late twenties – in the United States, such that they come to share in Christ's vision and take on "a mentality of faith" that will endure. First, I consider the cultural phenomenon of religious disaffiliation and suggest why it is understandable among young people. Second, I identify factors in the U.S. cultural imagination that challenge religious belief and belonging. Finally, I make three recommendations for effective catechesis among young people.

Affiliation and the Freedom to Leave

In the United States, religious faith and affiliation are increasingly in question. The Pew Research Forum's ongoing *Religious Landscape Study* reports that the percentage of Americans who are unaffiliated (22.8%) is greater than the percentage of Catholics (20.8%). The unaffiliated identify as atheist (3.1%), agnostic (4%), and "nothing in particular" (15.8%). The study reports that young adolescents largely follow the religious example of their parents, but their affiliation is weak and dependent on the parent's direction. Which suggests that once they are on their own, it is unlikely their affiliation will endure.

The growing body of research on religious affiliation finds that the major moment for disaffiliation occurs as a young person moves into adolescence and emerging adulthood.[1] This age of disaffiliation corresponds with a dramatic growth in cognitive capacity that occurs across the long span from childhood toward adulthood, which I outline in my book *Navigating toward Adulthood*. As a person moves from childhood, he or she is able to progress beyond the more concrete and immediate cognitive limits of later childhood and make sense of the world in increasingly complex ways. In particular, the adolescent grows the ability to see and think about the

[1] See Christian Smith, Kyle Longest, Jonathan Hill, and Kari Christoffersen, *Young Catholic America: Emerging Adults In, Out of, and Gone from the Church* (New York, NY: Oxford University Press, 2014); Robert McCarty and John Vitek, *Going, Going, Gone: The Dynamics of Disaffiliation in Young Catholic* (Winona, MN: St. Mary's Press, 2017).

world in terms of meaning, value, intention, and long term consequence. With appropriate support and challenge, this capacity for complex thought increases as he or she moves toward adulthood.

This cognitive transformation brings about two shifts that are significant to religious faith and affiliation. First, as they mature, adolescents are more insistent that things in their world make sense to them. For example, while the older child accepts going along with what seem to be arbitrary religious rules, stories, and practices directed by religious communities, adolescents become more frustrated and impatient with them. Adolescents expect that things make sense (i.e., logically or scientifically) if they are going to continue doing them. Given the opportunity, they will stop doing practices that seem arbitrary, especially if they impede their self-interest. On the other hand, if the reasons do make sense (e.g., they appreciate the value intended in a moral injunction), they will not only follow these practices, they will do so, even when doing so goes against self-interest. They may even become advocates and spokespersons for these practices with others.

A second factor of this transformation in cognitive capacity is the new awareness of social connections and their importance. Previously, affiliation was simply a matter of circumstance (e.g., if the parent goes to church, the child goes to church). With adolescence comes the ability to recognize the meaning and value in relationships and social membership (e.g., if going to church seems generally unpopular, they will want to stop going). The adolescent may drop unattractive or disadvantageous connections, but strengthen valuable ones. However, the maturing adolescent will maintain and strengthen a connection he or she finds personally valuable, even if it is unpopular. As the adolescent's agency grows over the years, he or she is increasingly able to determine with whom to affiliate or not.

If we hope that those in later adolescence, emerging adulthood and young adulthood come to "feel, think, and act like Christ" (§ 77) we need a catechesis that recognizes this cognitive shift and greater agency around affiliation. Rather than repeat the lessons of childhood or presume ongoing membership, the catechetical "game" must be elevated to meet and enhance the new abilities of the maturing person. Catechesis should be intentional about giving "a complete meaning to their existence" (§ 77) as well as pointing to the value of religious belonging for them as maturing persons. This clearly is a tall order.

An Obscured Horizon

Within Chapter X, the *Directory* identifies global cultural phenomena that affect the catechetical task. In his chapter in this collection, Hosffman Ospino offers a valuable analysis of culture and catechesis. I wish to highlight three cultural factors that I believe obscure a vision of an ultimate horizon, or a sense of the transcendent, among Christians in the United States. One factor is a view of God that is too small, but assumed to be the God of the Christian faith (cf. Pew Research Center, *Religious Landscape Study* 2021). Sometimes this god is not seen as the ultimate source of all life, but limited to the world of religion and spirituality, with no influence in other realms (e.g., science, politics, and the economy). Alternatively, this god created and set the world in motion, but has since stepped aside. Or this god favors some, but finds the majority of the human population unworthy of dignity and care. Regardless of how the particular belief takes shape, very often the god functioning in our cultural imagination is disconnected from or ineffectual to the realities of our lives. In the end, the god of the cultural imagination is too small and unworthy of further inquiry or wonder.

A second factor is the diversity of beliefs espoused by different religious traditions within the U.S. The *Directory* acknowledges this diversity, stating "the encounter with different religions has changed the way Christians live the experience of faith, opening believers to the question concerning the truth of the contents of the faith and freedom of choice" (§ 349). As contrary as it may seem, Christian faith in the God of Jesus Christ is not challenged by a deep inquiry into or understanding of another religious tradition. In fact, deep inquiry into the religious other usually results in a renewed appreciation for the distinctive gifts of Christianity.[2] Rather, the unstudied *presumption* that

---

2   See Theresa A. O'Keefe, "Relationships across the Divide: An Instigator of Transformation," *Studies in Christian-Jewish Relations*, 5, no. 1 (2010). https://doi.org/10.6017/scjr.v5i1.1553.

there is no real difference among religious traditions challenges faith in the God of Jesus Christ; it suggests that it does not matter what you believe. This too results in a benign disregard for further inquiry and wonder. The presumption of sameness distracts one from looking to the Christian horizon to inquire whether it calls forth anything unique, particular, and valuable. It obscures the meaningfulness of the God of Jesus Christ.

Finally, as a culture we are less concerned about life after death. Less than a century ago, most Christians believed in life after death. For their part, many Catholics believed St. Peter literally held the keys to the kingdom and that membership within the Catholic Church was a prerequisite for entrance into eternal life. Concern for one's eternal reward created a significant incentive for affiliation. Whereas today most U.S. Christians still believe in heaven, most think that entrance requirements are not very high (cf. *Religious Landscape Study*). Furthermore, for young people, many who may expect to live at least another 50 years, concern about life after death does not have much immediacy. As a result, concern for one's immortal soul is a far less compelling incentive for church affiliation than it once was.

Generations ago, Christian religious belief and affiliation were intelligible and valued givens of the U.S. landscape. On the other hand, the three factors named each reflect a waning interest today among U.S. Christians in religious teachings about God and transcendence. Christian religious faith seems more and more archaic, especially to many young people. If religious faith does not matter, then religious affiliation matters even less. These sentiments about religious belief and belonging only exacerbate the challenge of catechizing adolescents, emerging, and young adults in the Catholic Church in the United States. This is a very different landscape than was encountered by Catholic leadership of previous generations, and calls for a different catechesis.

A Path toward the Horizon

One possible response to these cultural and developmental realities is to limit the catechetical task by circling the wagons into an ever-smaller community of those who already believe and belong.

Another response, as the *Directory* suggests, is to recognize the link between catechesis and evangelization – even among the baptized – and catechize in a way that opens "a new horizon of life... starting with the encounter with the Lord Jesus" (§ 55). Put another way, in the U.S. context, we should approach catechesis as if those we meet do not fully know how the Catholic Church names the God of Jesus Christ, do not know how that belief offers meaning and direction for their lives, and have not yet recognized the value of church affiliation. For this reason, catechesis needs to be *meaningful, accessible*, and *compelling*. I believe this is particularly true for the Church's catechetical witness with adolescents, emerging, and young adults, who are increasingly able to think critically about how they identify and with whom they affiliate.

A Meaningful Horizon

Catechesis is not about sharing insider secrets for an obscure club, otherwise disconnected from reality. Rather catechesis is the effort of shaping people into a way of seeing life – all life. The *Directory* speaks of it as "a dynamic and complex reality at the service of the Word of God, it is accompaniment, education, and formation in the faith for the faith, an introduction to the celebration of the Mystery, illumination and interpretation of human life and history" (§ 55). As young people grow in their capacity to understand the world, it is important that catechesis present the Christian faith as offering a way of interpreting life – its source, its meaning, and its direction. Yet this interpretation is not primarily didactic. Through all the tools available (e.g., scripture, liturgy, social engagement, prayer, community), catechesis shares and shapes followers in a vision of life's ultimate horizon – the love of God.

For that horizon to be meaningful to young people, it is necessary not only to communicate *what* the Church teaches, but also *why* it teaches and *how* that teaching matters. Catechesis is to help people to come to see their lives and the world "in a mentality of faith, in keeping with the Gospel, to the point of gradually coming to feel, think and act like Christ" (§ 77). To help young people discover the deep meaning within the Church's teaching, catechesis must connect the dots, so that Church doctrine "can be used as a reference in life" (§ 80). Practices and injunctions should appear less arbitrary and more grounded in deep meaning and hope. As Patrick Manning articulates in his chapter in this collection, catechesis shapes the imagination. Catechesis must communicate a wide horizon of God's creating and saving love, active in the world, and help young people discern that horizon in all situations.

The catechetical goal of "forming persons who get to know Jesus Christ and his Gospel of liberating salvation even better" constantly invites young people to seek Jesus' presence everywhere. (§ 75). For example, the Catholic Church's teaching on abortion, immigration, racism, health care, systemic poverty, and migration are not isolated and arbitrary teachings. A vision of the human person, created in love by God, links them all. Each human person is full of innate dignity, which circumstance does not alter. Therefore, in myriad ways, catechesis must communicate what it means to us that God created all things, visible and invisible and the influence it has on how we interpret our world.

An Accessible Map

In part, catechesis means accessibly translating between the Church's language of faith and the language of the local context. Unfortunately, most documents, like the *Directory* and the *Catechism of the Catholic Church*, use what amounts to coded (Catholic) language, assuming readers understand it. Neither is immediately accessible, nor are they intended as such. However, catechesis, especially with young people, needs to be accessible. The *Directory* states there is a "pressing need for ... translating the message of Jesus into [young people's] language" (§ 245). Clearly, technical terms, such as *incarnation* and *sacrament*, are obscure and rich with meaning; catechesis needs to explain them in multiple ways to expand a young person's understanding. Yet, even more familiar words, like *God* and *love*, have much deeper and different meanings within the Christian tradition than are common in the culture. On a very basic level, catechesis needs to expand Christian concepts so they are both distinct and understandable. This is not to suggest learners are unintelligent, rather that they may not share the same vocabulary and understanding.

Subject matter must also be accessible. The *Directory* states, "The experience of individuals or of society as a whole must be approached with an attitude of love, acceptance and respect. God acts in every person's life and in history, and the catechist imitates Jesus in being open to this presence" (§ 197). Catechesis needs to approach the faith in a manner that pertains to the embodied life and perspective of the young person, rather than from ecclesial leaders. In the preparation process for the 2018 Synod "Young People, Faith, and Vocational Discernment," Church leaders learned that young people are particularly concerned about issues of justice, especially as so many young people suffer amid poverty, exploitation, discrimination, and anxiety. They are looking to the Church to lead in advocacy on the concerns they face. The U.S. Catholic Church needs to both listen and add its voice on issues such as systemic racism, wealth inequality, immigration, and housing. The *Directory* states, "An integral part of the journey of exploration of the faith is the development of a social and political vision attentive to the elimination of injustices, to the building up of peace and the safeguarding of creation, to the promotion of various forms of solidarity and subsidiarity" (§ 389). The Church can catechize by investigating these issues with young people and interpreting the Church's teachings in light of them. Young people are looking to the Church to rise above the political battles to offer guidance and thoughtful engagement around social and political issues. Catechesis is not simply an act of telling, but also accompaniment, inviting young people to share their vision of God's loving action in the world.

A Compelling Community

Finally, our lives, as well as our words, offer a compelling catechesis. The *Directory* posits that young people "need to have convinced and compelling witnesses by their side" (§ 249). Christian faith is not a solo effort. To live in the belief of God's ongoing love and presence requires a community that informs and sustains that vision. The community is the "locus" of catechesis (§ 133). It serves as an accessible witness to the meaningfulness of the vision it holds, even when immediate circumstances obscure that vision. In her chapter in this collection, Susanna Singer identifies multiple ways this can happen. As the community stands as a model of God's love, it draws people to itself and to God.

Throughout, the *Directory* makes the important point that "The laity, in bearing witness to the Gospel in different contexts, have the opportunity to give a Christian interpretation to the realities of life, to speak of Christ and of Christian values, to present the reasons for their choices" (§ 121). It identifies "accompaniment" and "articulation" as essential to catechesis (§§ 55, 113, 132). Pastoral leaders need to create spaces within which relationships might flourish, especially among young people and mature adults. In such spaces, members can help one another as guides, interpreting life in light of the horizon of God's love. Through these efforts of accompaniment and articulation, the catechetical experience itself becomes an encounter with Christ.

In *Christus Vivit*, Pope Francis writes "Young

people need to be approached with the grammar of love... by those who are there for them and with them. And those who, for all their limitations and weaknesses, try to live their faith with integrity" (§ 212). Catechesis is in part an intellectual task, "fostering knowledge of the Creed and the creation of a coherent doctrinal vision that can be used as a reference in life" (§ 80). However, the *Directory* makes clear in multiple ways, the Catholic Christian faith is not a set of obscure tenets; it is an encounter with Christ. This encounter translates into a way of seeing all life as constantly created, blessed and redeemed by God. We believe this not because it is empirically provable or reasonably argued, rather, we believe this because of the compelling faith lived in community. This truth shapes our imaginations such that we come to recognize God's loving presence in all ways and at all times, even when circumstances obscure it. Catechesis that is meaningful, accessible and compelling is essential to share this vision.

Questions for Conversation:
1 How does your belief in Christ or God help you make sense of your life? How would you speak of that experience with someone who does not does not share your understanding of and relationship to Christianity?
2 What aspects of membership in a faith community are important to you? How would you express that with someone who has not had your experience?

Recommended Readings:
Pope Francis. *Christus Vivit*, Post-Synodal Apostolic Exhortation to Young People and to the Entire People of God (2019).

Theresa A. O'Keefe. *Navigating toward Adulthood: A Theology of Ministry with Adolescents*. New York: Paulist, 2018.

Patrick B. Reyes. *Nobody Cries When We Die: God, Community, and Surviving to Adulthood*. St. Louis, MO: Chalice Press, 2016.

9
Catechesis and Digital Culture
Daniella Zsupan-Jerome

Facilitating a living encounter with Christ (§ 75). Every seasoned catechist knows that throughout all the planning, scheduling, meetings, presentations, retreats, filling out the proper forms and getting copies of the proper certificates, at the heart of catechetical ministry is but this one central task. Catechists help guide people to Christ, to meet Christ in a *living encounter*, which in turn gives life to each seeker in a new and profound way. Everything else in the practice of catechesis is built around this.

Encounter is an essential concept not only to catechesis but also to the church's approach to ministry and the broader culture, including digital culture (Pope Francis, *Evangelii Gaudium*, 87-91). We all have countless experiences of encounters throughout life– some are fleeting, some are lengthy, some are mundane, some are life-changing. In today's world, more and more we are encountering one another in mediated ways in various digital spaces. In this digital culture, we experience our encounters with one another increasingly through gadgets and screens of all shapes and sizes. When ministers reflect on facilitating a living encounter with Christ, we may rightly wonder how our daily encounters of the digital kind shape our understanding of this most sacred goal of catechesis. In a digital culture where so many of our interactions are mediated by screens and gadgets, how do we enter into authentic, living, life-changing encounters, above all with Christ but also with one another as members of his Body? This question is important for the church and for catechesis as a formative process that seeks to shape minds and hearts, and build communities in the image of Christ. This chapter offers a reflection on catechesis along these lines, focusing on opportunities and challenges of this new reality we call digital culture. Rather than suggesting specific tools and gadgets or even a detailed list of "how to do digital catechesis," the invitation here is to recognize and reflect on how our world has shifted as a whole and what impact this has on catechesis today and moving forward.

What is Digital Culture? Positives and Negatives

The *Directory for Catechesis* (henceforth, *Directory*) is astute in its assessment of digital culture as "a culture." As it notes, when we reflect on life in digital culture, we are no longer just talking about the presence of technological means, but how our contemporary world has changed as a whole (§ 359). Digital culture is a term that points beyond the fact that we have innovative new communication technologies available to us. Rather, it is a term that refers to particular thought patterns, behaviors, values, artifacts, and linguistic expressions that we commonly hold as a result of the impact of the communication technology available to us. Living in digital culture means we have in recent decades experienced a tremendous cultural shift through which we have come to hold new assumptions about what it means to interact and communicate with one another, to gain access to resources and information, and to participate in public discourse in formal and informal ways. This cultural shift has in many ways been positive. Because of the communication technology available to us, we have extraordinary opportunities for dialogue, encounter and exchange between persons as well as access to information and knowledge (§ 360). The convenience of our smartphones and all to which it can provide easy access is staggering to think about, especially when compared to our daily life just a few decades ago. Technology has enabled new conveniences, but more importantly, it has also engendered in us a total mental shift toward a new way of living our daily lives as we enjoy these conveniences. The *Directory* uses the term *digital enhancements* to define the ways these technological conveniences have become an extension and enrichment of our human capacities (§ 360). More and more we offload our tasks to these digital enhancements, which in turn is shaping our general approach to everyday life. This is truly a cultural shift, that includes new ways of thought, new assumptions, new values, new linguistic expressions, new behaviors and new artifacts, which together comprise what we call digital culture.

Digital culture may have arisen out of the conveniences and life-enhancements from innovative communication technologies. At the same time, this culture has also ushered in some notable challenges. While we have the extraordinary opportunity for dialogue, encounter and exchange, we also may fall into loneliness, manipulation, exploitation, false information, cyberbullying and verbal violence, addiction, distortion of reality and a general disregard of the inherent dignity of human persons (§ 361). Digital technologies may bring us into deeper communion with one another, or they may lead us further apart, marring our dignity and sapping our lives. While these technologies seem like powerful entities of their own, in digital culture we are still embedded in what Pope Francis refers to as an environment rich in humanity, a "network not of wires but of people" (*World Communications Day Message 2014: Communications at the Service of an Authentic Culture of Encounter*). In other words, it is up to the human person, with the help of grace, to shape our digital culture into a life-giving context toward communion. We are at a crossroad as we may rise or fall in this new digitally connected world. For catechesis as a formation process toward fullness of life in Christ, this crossroad offers a supremely relevant opportunity.

A Living Encounter in Culture and in Catechesis
Catechesis fosters a living encounter with Christ, and at the same time forms believers to gain a deep and meaningful sense of what an encounter is, with God and with others. One of the core challenges of digital culture, underpinning many of the problems listed above, is that we often forget about the encounters we are experiencing online as *actual encounters with people*. What feels like a solitary moment with a gadget is in reality an instance in a crowded public square. The screen mediates the real presence of actual people by reducing them to electronically rendered text, image and sound, conveyed across space and time. Once a person is reduced to this representation, it becomes much easier to reify an encounter into an experience of merely accessing information on a screen. Once we forget that there is a person there, we run the risk of forgetting the humanity of digital culture.

Catechesis, a ministry of the word built around the living encounter with Christ, faces a formidable opportunity here. Catechesis accompanies believers through a living encounter with Christ, who in turn extend this experience of encounter to members of the ecclesial community and beyond. A living encounter with Christ and the church leads to conversion, gives life, builds communion, and more. In the context of digital culture, though, a living encounter through catechesis redefines what encounter is and presents a standard of authenticity for the encounter-experience. For digital culture, this means that catechetical formation has the potential not only to foster *metanoia* in individual believers, but instead to transform culture through the faithful presence of disciples who communicate with intention, dignity and a sense of communion. Catechesis in this sense can extend awareness of the living encounter with Christ throughout culture, especially digital culture.

Along these lines, catechesis offers to digital culture a standard for deeper and more authentic human interactions. This is an immense gift vis-à-vis "the progressive dehumanization" that can emerge as a real threat in digital culture (§ 361). Catechesis in this sense truly accompanies persons who are well aware of the dehumanizing aspects of the digital world which we inhabit. A catechesis of encounter brings the Good News into the heart of this reality and gives us a more human way of approaching digital communication. Through the lens of catechesis, we seek and expect more, thus bringing glimpses of communion into a context that functions well enough just on a vast network of connections.

What Catechesis Can Learn from Digital Culture
While catechesis bears this gift for digital culture, the relationship between catechesis and digital culture is open both ways. In fact, catechesis itself is embedded in the digital culture that pervades our reality today. Along these lines, the *Directory* accurately notes that a key question for catechesis is "how to become an evangelizing presence on the digital continent" (§ 371). This means that catechesis exists in the midst of these cultural realities, not apart from it while "beaming in" religious information. Embedded in digital culture, the task for catechesis is to

"understand the power of this medium and to use all its potentialities and positive aspects, while still realizing that catechesis cannot be carried out solely by using digital tools but by offering spaces for experiences of faith" (§ 371). This calls for keen awareness of both the gifts and the challenges of digital culture and striving to help people experience God in the context of these. Informing about religion or offering religious instruction is only a part of this; a significant part that needs to be rounded out by an accompanying presence that welcomes people into community and communion.

If catechesis exists in the midst of digital culture and seeks to accompany people therein, there are important ways that digital culture itself may have an impact on catechesis. For example, sharing information in digital culture is characteristically visual image driven, as opposed to lengthy text or even sound. When perusing one's social media feed, pictures, gifs (graphic interface format images), memes, emojis and videos dominate. When discerning how to accompany people and present opportunities for experiencing faith, this dominant communication form compels catechesis to tell the story of faith in a resonant way. Lengthy text, a hallmark of so much of the modern Christian intellectual tradition, struggles to tell the story of faith in this visual world. In order to reveal the richness of the tradition, a new pedagogy for digital culture calls forth the rich visual tradition of Christianity in a new, creative and inspired way. Timothy O'Malley's chapter on the language of the arts and the formative nature of liturgy in this collection reminds us of how much communication of faith is possible beyond the text.

Another impact of digital culture on catechesis is new assumptions about who the communicators of faith are today. In digital culture, using one's voice and participating in social discourse is elemental to life today: anyone with a smartphone in their hand can do so. Voice and participation may range from mundane, lighthearted to meaningful and profound; the point is not so much the content as having a voice that contributes. For catechesis, forming disciples who share the Good News, this impetus to communicate offers a solid foundation to build upon. The task of catechesis in this regard is to form believers to become communicators *of the faith* in the midst of the digital flow. Participation and voice in digital culture thus offers catechesis a new opportunity for evangelization. For example, on social media, many people of faith readily post or comment on content of faith, from inspirational images and quotes to thoughtful articles and videos exploring a topic. Even prayerful comments one adds under a posting about life, love, or loss is an aspect of sharing one's faith. Catechesis can guide this impetus to share one's faith to be more intentional, informed and dialogical.

Practical Recommendations

Catechesis is at once firmly rooted in divine revelation, and evolving with respect to the cultures and contexts in which the Word of God is uttered. Digital culture is a new cultural context which calls for the shaping of a new catechesis that is able to accompany people today and facilitate a living encounter with Christ in the midst of our screen-saturated world. Along these lines, a new catechesis for the digital world should be especially attentive to two areas: listening and participation. Attentiveness to these two helps catechesis to take practical steps with digital culture in mind.

Listening

As the *Directory* points out, the overwhelmingly visual focus of digital culture diminishes the opportunity for listening (§ 363). The rapid and constant flow of information does not readily lend itself to slow, attentive and careful consideration. Ongoing consumption of rapid-fire information without the invitation to truly listen leaves an impoverished experience of communication, which can become isolating and dehumanizing over time. Catechesis has the opportunity to introduce another way of communication.

Listening is a fundamental hospitality within us to God and to others. It is at the heart of a vibrant spiritual life, as well as healthy interpersonal relationships. Without listening we create echo chambers and experience increasing isolation and atrophy over time. Catechesis is built on the practice of listening, and thus is at a prime place to attend to this broader cultural need. In practical terms, a new catechesis for digital culture will value and insist on a practice of listening and careful attentiveness as part of the formative process. Exercises that invite slow, deliberate engagement with the word, such as *lectio divina* or Scripture study are excellent counterbalances to the rapid engagement with words we are used to on the screen. Important also is the pace and pattern of group conversations in the catechetical setting. Group conversations in and of themselves have formative potential especially if the group is intentional about engaging in good communication skills, including listening and attentiveness to others. A practical way to achieve this is to discuss, model and invite participants to assent to a particular pattern of group communication at the group's initial gathering. In addition to intentional listening, this pattern may include respect for confidentiality, safe space for conversation, respectful dialogue over differences, using I-statements and more. In these ways, catechesis as a ministry of the word invites participants to experience communication in a godly way, creating a formative process that brings balance to digital culture.

The concept of listening also has much to offer for fostering a faithful presence in the digital spaces themselves. Slowing down, asking genuine questions, interpreting generously and engaging in dialogue are almost countercultural postures when it comes to today's social media comment feed, where the tenor of the exchanges very quickly escalates to conflict and verbal violence. Catechesis can offer a formative space in which a different kind of conversation happens, based on authentic listening and hospitality to the other. Lakisha Lockhart's chapter in this collection demonstrates the importance of such hospitality in catechesis which one's total experience is welcome and respected. Such an experience of hospitality can in turn form our online exchanges, especially those that share faith, to become a witness for a conversation toward encounter rather than conflict.

Participation

As noted above, in our digital culture, having a voice and participating in social discourse is an elemental part of life. Catechesis can capitalize on this by reinforcing the call to evangelization and fostering a faithful use of the public voice. In practical terms, it is good practice along these lines to ask participants to express and share their thoughts regularly as part of the catechetical process. A banking or solely lecture-based model of catechetical instruction is less helpful in this regard than a method rooted in discussion. The more that a participant learns to use his or her public voice of faith, the better.

Along with fostering more conversation as part of the pedagogical process, catechesis in digital culture may also be more attentive to how the meaningful contribution of each participant is honored as part of the overall curriculum, and indeed, the broader culture of the church. In a participatory culture such as our digital one, members gain a strong sense of belonging through the experience that their presence and contribution is valued and matters.[1]

---

[1] See Henry Jenkins, Ravi Purushotma, Margaret Weigel, Katie Clinton, and Alice Robison, *Confronting the Challenges of Participatory Culture: Media Education for the 21st Century* (Cambridge, MA: MIT Press, 2009), 7.

Whether lighthearted or serious, people continue to contribute online because of the recognition, feedback, likes and comments that communicate to them that their presence and story matters. It is important for catechesis and the broader church to reflect on the extent to which this is true in the culture of the church. Some practical steps for catechesis in this direction include inviting experience and storytelling into the overall conversation, asking for and honoring feedback from participants, and emphasizing the baptismal identity and vocation of participants in content and in practice.

The concept of participation also speaks to how to establish a digital presence as part of ministry. In order to establish a vibrant digital presence for ministry, participation is in fact the key. This means that digital ministry should first and foremost invite the participation of *a team* of people to plan, lead and administer the digital presence. This is an excellent opportunity to form a diverse, intergenerational group who collaborate with pastoral leadership toward conveying a vibrant presence in the digital space.

In addition, a significant question for digital ministry to consider is to what extent to invite the active, visible and public participation of those who may come across the digital presence of the ministry online. Are comments and contributions invited, and from whom? Can people become co-creators of the story the digital ministry is telling online or are they a more passive "audience"? What are the practical administrative details behind the scenes for welcoming public comments and who will be responsible for overseeing these? These are a few questions to keep in mind when considering the implications of participation on a public scale for digital ministry.

Through new experiences of digital communication, we are living in the midst of an immense cultural shift. As communication continues to change the world, catechesis, as a ministry of the word, is especially well-poised to discern the movement of the Spirit and follow in step with creativity, enthusiasm and a profound sense of possibility, forming disciples to live the Good News in digital culture. Catechesis, if intentional about accompanying people today, can guide us from merely enjoying digital enhancements to fullness of life lived toward encounter and communion.

Questions for Conversation:
1 What are the "potentialities and positive aspects" of digital culture? In what way do these matter for catechesis?
2 How have you experienced faith in and through digital culture? How might you help create an experience of faith in the context of digital culture?

Recommended Readings:
Pope Francis. "Communication at the Service of an Authentic Culture of Encounter." Message for the 48th World Communications Day, June 1, 2014. Available at www.vatican.va

Pope John Paul II. "The Rapid Development." Apostolic Letter to those responsible for communications, January 24, 2005. Available at www.vatican.va

Daniella Zsupan-Jerome. *Connected Toward Communion: The Church and Social Communication in the Digital Age*. Collegeville, MN: Liturgical Press, 2014.

10
Shaping a Meaningful Vision for Life in Today's World
Patrick R. Manning

"The definitive aim of catechesis is to put people not only in touch but in communion, in intimacy, with Jesus Christ: only He can lead us to the love of the Father in the Spirit and make us share in the life of the Holy Trinity" (Pope John Paul II, *Catechesi Tradendae*, §5). Whatever else might be going on in our parishes, schools, and the wider world, these words serve as a beacon to draw us back to the proper focus of catechesis, namely, the love of the Father, friendship with Jesus, and "fullness of life" in the Spirit and in communion with one another (John 10:10).

This goal is both simple and difficult. Jesus made it clear: "I am the way and the truth and the life" (John 14:6). Yet the apostles struggled to follow Jesus even with the benefit of knowing him in the flesh. Living at a remove of 2,000 years adds another layer of challenge for contemporary disciples. As times change, Christians have to figure out how to follow

Jesus within their particular context. Catechists likewise have to read the "signs of the times" in order to support disciples' efforts to grow in communion with Christ in this particular time and place (§ 42; cf. § 44).

The New Shape of the Timeless Goal

Among the features of the contemporary world noted in the new *Directory for Catechesis* (henceforth, *Directory*) are "profound changes... taking place within the *horizon of meaning* of human experience itself" (§ 46). Mass media and social media, the advertising and entertainment industrial complex, globalization, and the mixing of races, religions, and cultures are among the factors overwhelming our capacity to make sense of the fragmented situations in which we find ourselves on a daily basis (§ 199). These complexities not only make it more difficult to navigate life in the day-to-day; as the *Directory* explains, they also affect our "cognitive capacities" and "the very approach to the experience of faith" (§ 47).

Virtually all of us have felt the impact of these changes in one way or another. Parents struggle to explain the value of Catholic teachings to their children when the wider culture and even personal acquaintances often contradict them. We feel overwhelmed and unmoored in the face of the busyness of life, rapid and momentous social and technological changes, and violence and economic instability around the world. Many of us in ministry have sat with young people through their bouts of anxiety and confusion. We have listened to them as they try to sort fact from fiction in news reports and social media posts and to find cause for hope as environmental predictions grow ever grimmer. Those of us who minister with and care deeply about these people cannot but be concerned by the yawning chasm between Christianity's vision for the life of humanity and their lived reality.

Recognizing how disorienting life in today's world can be, the *Directory* emphasizes that an important function of catechesis is helping Christians "to give a complete meaning to their existence" (§ 77). How the *Directory* describes this happening is significant (and pragmatic): not merely by transmitting information (§ 371) but more profoundly by forming the catechized in a *"mentality of faith* in keeping with the Gospel, to the point of gradually coming to feel, think and act like Christ" (§ 77). To be well catechized in this understanding is to have internalized the church's teachings not just as propositions to be affirmed but more holistically as a vision for life, a lens through which one views reality in all its dimensions (§ 80). It is to nurture what theologians call a religious imagination.

What characterizes this mentality of faith or Christian imagination in a person? People formed in this way possess a solid sense of Christian identity, recognizing themselves as bearers of the divine image and beloved children of God. Likewise, they see the same divine image in everyone else (even difficult coworkers and political adversaries). In their daily dealings, they see the value of people over material goods, efficiency, and profits. With the image of the cross fixed in their memory, they expect to see God bring good even out of misfortunes like losing a job or a global pandemic. Such were the contours of Jesus' vision of reality and of those who have followed after him through the ages.

Faith for Today's World

Although these features of the Christian imagination remain constant today as in the past, life in today's world demands that Christians' imagining take on new dimensions as well. So what does it look like to have a mentality or imagination that is not only authentically Christian but also commensurate with contemporary existential situations, marked as they often are by new challenges and complexities (§ 77)? This is a crucial question for catechetical leaders to be asking because, in order to prepare Christians for faithful living in contemporary society, catechists must identify and cultivate the *capacities* demanded of disciples in today's world. Fortunately, the *Directory* provides helpful guidance in this regard.

First, a mentality of faith commensurate with the contemporary situation is one that is personally owned and deliberately nurtured. Living in an increasingly pluralistic and secular society, the majority of Catholics no longer passively absorb a Christian worldview or Catholic answers to the questions of life, as Theresa O'Keefe argues in her chapter in this collection. Many struggle mightily with questions about who they are, the meaning of their lives, and what morals to live by and pass on to their children. They often bear the burden of answering these questions alone (or feel that they do).

The implication for contemporary catechesis, as the *Directory* notes, is that in such a context it is crucial "to help each individual to develop his own unique response of faith" (§ 3). Most basically this means presenting personal faith as a task for Catholics to undertake intentionally and persistently. The big questions of life and faith sit on the backburner in the minds of many Catholics who feel consumed with more immediate matters and perhaps even busy themselves so they do not have to confront these big questions. By contrast, the modern-day disciples who are thriving in today's world are often those who consciously and intentionally work to make sense of their experiences and the world they encounter. They regularly reflect with others and on their own about how God might be at work in whatever is going on in their lives. They pay attention to how social media, advertising, and popular entertainment shape the meaning from which they live, including the ways they think about faith. They examine their lifestyle and commit to practices that help them to feel, think, and act like Christ (e.g., keeping a day of Sabbath rest each week, discerning small and big decisions, and honoring the body).[1] Finally and crucially, they seek out friends and community who will support them in this work. In this way, they discover in the Catholic Tradition answers to life's big questions and develop a vision that guides their lives. They don't always have all the answers, but they do see that there is meaning to be found and that provides enough light to illuminate a path forward.

This leads to the second feature of this contemporary mentality of faith. A Christian imagination commensurate with the challenges of the day is necessarily an *active* imagination. In today's world we are compelled to adapt to constant change and a relentless flood of information, data, images, and messages, as Daniella Zsupan-Jerome lays out in her chapter in this collection. These novel

---

1 See Dorothy Bass, ed., *Practicing Our Faith: A Way of Life for a Searching People* (Minneapolis, MN: Fortress Press, 2019).

elements of modern society have changed not only the way our brains work but also the way we develop as psycho-social beings (§ 47, 257). With so much information and so many novelties bombarding us on a daily basis, a static understanding of faith is doomed to quickly come to be perceived as antiquated and irrelevant (and indeed this is how many young people now see it). "This is the reason why the present *Directory* reiterates the importance of having catechesis accompany the development of a *mentality of faith* in a dynamic of *transformation*" (§ 3).

Like modern buildings and bridges built with the flexibility to withstand earthquakes and high winds, those Christian disciples who are flourishing in today's world exhibit a mentality of faith that is adaptive and resilient. When new scientific discoveries or the perspectives of other religions and cultures challenge their beliefs, they do not plug their ears or rehearse old arguments to justify themselves. They listen, question, and learn. They go back to the wellsprings of faith—the stories and symbols of Scripture, the liturgy, and prayer—in search of a deeper meaning, and they do this time and time again. This sort of active imagination is what enables them to grow in understanding of the world and their faith, to live gracefully into new circumstances rather than clinging to a past that no longer exists, and to interact with others with openness and generosity rather than becoming defensive and disconnected.

Catechesis That Meets the Challenges of Today

If this is the kind of Christian mentality or imagination demanded by life in today's world, what kind of catechesis is required to nurture such a mentality of faith? Equipping disciples for faithful living in the modern world will require a two-fold paradigm shift: one aspect concerning pedagogy and the other concerning community life.

The first (pedagogical) paradigm shift involves truly treating the catechized as "active participants," as people actively working to make sense of faith rather than passive receptacles for information or robots to be programmed (§ 4; cf. §§ 3, 332). Treating people like meaning-makers requires understanding how we make meaning and supporting this work deliberately in catechetical contexts. Constructing meaning (including meaningful faith) is a complex enterprise, but for simplicity's sake, we can identify three components that appear prominently in both psychological research and the *Directory*: experiencing, questioning, and judging.

Experiencing

Our experiences—along with the mental images we form from these experiences—provide the raw material from which we construct meaning. For this reason, it is vital that catechists pay attention to the learners' personal experiences, especially when working with young people for whom experience (rather than authority, tradition, doctrine) is frequently the "default mediator of meaning and truth."[2] Doctrine is meaningless to them if they don't see the connection to their personal experiences—to the daily realities of school and work, their suffering,

---

2   Robert McCarty and John Vitek, *Going, Going, Gone: The Dynamics of Disaffiliation in Young Catholic* (Winona, MN: St. Mary's Press, 2017), 24.

their relationships. The new *Directory* affirms that human experience is "a primary form of mediation for getting to the truth of Revelation" (§ 200). Catechists can help the catechized to recognize God within their own experiences by, for example, giving learners opportunities to talk and write about their lives, discussing the videos they watch and the music they listen to, and inviting them to give expression (in conversation, writing, artwork) to the way they see things.

Although personal experience is inevitably the starting point and foundation for meaning, it is limited and limiting if not expanded by dialogue with other perspectives. Expanding horizons is one benefit of engaging the Catholic Tradition, which bears 2,000 years' worth of wisdom and God's own self-revelation. If catechesis fails to have an effect on learners, it is frequently because catechists present the Tradition merely as a repository of ideas rather than facilitating an *experience* or, in the words of Pope Benedict XVI, an "encounter with an event, a person, which gives life a new horizon and a decisive direction" (*Deus Caritas Est*, § 1). Again recognizing this reality, the *Directory* emphasizes the importance of "paying attention to the symbols, gestures, and ceremonies of the liturgy and of popular piety... that more easily [touch] the human heart" (§ 353). See Timothy O'Malley's chapter in this collection for more on liturgy. Elsewhere the *Directory* mentions stories and images and "above all the witness of saints and catechists" (§ 164). Indeed, there is no more effective catechesis than the witness of a Christian whose very being manifests what it looks like to be fully alive and inflamed with the love of God. Direct service with the poor, imaginative reading of Scripture in the Ignatian tradition, and engaged forms of prayer like labyrinth walking or Taizé-style services are other ways catechists can give learners a meaningful experience of the Tradition and perhaps even of God.

Questioning
Of course, it is entirely possible to have the experience but miss the meaning, as T.S. Eliot once wrote. Experience of the Tradition translates into meaningful faith when we seek to understand the

experience, when we ask questions about it and search for answers. For this reason the *Directory* encourages catechists to adopt "a humble willingness to allow oneself to be touched by the questions and confronted by the situations of life" (§ 132). Young people have earnest questions about identity, sexuality, suffering, death, the natural world, and many other topics. When learners pose such questions, catechists ought to afford them due respect and ample space for exploration. To brush them off or provide a pat answer in order to get back to the lesson plan is to miss an opportunity when their charges are open to meaningful learning and to risk sending the (erroneous) message that Catholicism lacks resources for answering life's biggest questions.

Judging

Beyond engaging experience, asking questions, and seeking answers, there remains a further, crucial step in the work of making sense of faith, namely, rendering personal judgments. A truth proclaimed by the church has little meaning for someone until they claim that truth for their own and act upon it (cf.

Matthew 7:24). Catechists may find it unnerving to expose church teaching to learners' criticisms and personal judgments. However, the *Directory* encourages us to recognize in this critical attitude "a valuable opportunity to make adherence to the Lord an act that is profoundly personal and gratuitous, mature and deliberate" (§ 322). The fact of the matter is that we have little choice. Young people are already making their own judgments upon church teaching—often by rejecting it. Either we invite them to make personal judgments in the catechetical setting where we can ask and answer further questions, or we leave them to make these judgments on their own. Practically speaking, inviting intentional judgments and decisions for faith involves things like building time into meetings for discussion of topics that still don't make sense to participants, creative projects in which learners synthesize what they have learned in a personal vision for their lives (e.g., an action plan or artistic project), and opportunities for putting that vision into action (e.g., by engaging in service or committing to new spiritual practices).

The impact of the pedagogical approach described above is greatly amplified when it is not merely the prerogative of catechists working in isolation but rather one aspect of a commitment on the part of the whole community to value, nurture, and practice a mature mentality of faith. This brings us to the second paradigm shift. We need Catholic parishes, schools, and families that can serve as communities of accompaniment (cf. § 132, 352). A community of accompaniment is a place where members are both supported and challenged, welcomed and provoked, a space where they can grapple with their struggles in faith, work through developmental transitions, and be held up when everything is falling to pieces around them (cf. § 160). Admittedly, this is difficult work. It makes us uncomfortable when people ask challenging questions and diverge from the norm. The temptation is to silence or push these people out. Unfortunately, this happens all too often in our Catholic communities, a tendency that has played no small part in the exodus of spiritual seekers and the intellectually curious.

If we are to be a community that is truly "catholic" (i.e., universal), if we are to prepare people to live their faith in an increasingly complex world, members of our Catholic communities—especially those in leadership roles—must develop the capacity to abide such tensions within themselves and to support (as well as challenge) those who elicit these tensions. This certainly includes catechists whose formation should include training in the "art of accompaniment" (§ 132). Looking beyond catechists to the community that surrounds them, one often finds that parishes who have succeeded in creating a culture of accompaniment have also cultivated mentors and small faith communities who walk with and support teenagers, young adults, and families as they grapple with the challenges particular to their stage on the journey of faith. When growth (and growing pains) are expected and patient accompaniment is the norm within a community, members are far more likely to experience Christian faith as living and life-giving.

In conclusion, consider the following three suggestions for nurturing the kind of mentality of faith needed for Catholics to live meaningful, faithful lives in contemporary society: First, treat learners like meaning-makers by deliberately and regularly engaging their personal life experiences, providing meaningful experiences of the Catholic Tradition (e.g., prayer, liturgy, stories, service), giving real attention to their questions, and inviting their personal judgments and decisions. Second, identify and empower people in your community who exhibit a mature mentality of faith. Invite them to serve in roles (e.g., mentor, catechist, retreat leader) where they can tell their story and model this mentality of faith. Finally, train catechists and mentors in the art of accompaniment. For example, you might use the U.S. Bishops' *Creating a Culture of Encounter* or form small faith sharing groups where catechists can meet regularly to discuss difficult questions and situations in the classroom and in their students' lives. Such ongoing conversation will prepare them to respond confidently to difficult questions and to be patient with students as they mature.

Questions for Conversation:

1 Where have you found meaning for your life? Where have you found meaning in the Catholic Tradition? How did you discover it? How might you help others to do likewise?
2 How welcoming is your parish/school/community of critical questions and perspectives? How might you capitalize upon such questions as opportunities for growth rather than reacting to them as threats?

Recommended Readings:

Sharon Daloz Parks. *Big Questions, Worthy Dreams: Mentoring Emerging Adults in Their Search for Meaning, Purpose, and Faith.* San Francisco, CA: Jossey-Bass, 2000.

Patrick R. Manning. *Converting the Imagination: Teaching to Recover Jesus' Vision for Fullness of Life.* Eugene, OR: Pickwick Publications, 2020.

United States Conference of Catholic Bishops. *Creating a Culture of Encounter: A Guide for Joyful*

Missionary Disciples. Washington, D.C.: USCCB, 2019.

11
The Parish as a Vital Space of Catechetical Formation
Susan Bigelow Reynolds

In March 2020, parishes across the nation shut down to help curb the spread of COVID-19. When the lockdown started, it only took my family two Sundays to realize that virtual Mass wasn't going to work. From the minute we fired up the livestream, our older daughters—then aged five and three—would moan, splay themselves across the floor, and eventually wander off to seek refuge in the playroom. They started insisting on "playing church" instead. The oldest appointed herself sacristan, repurposing her craft table into an altar, digging through the linen cabinet for a tablecloth in the appropriate liturgical color, retrieving candlesticks from the mantle, and taking the crucifix off the wall. Her younger sister led an opening procession around our kitchen. We sang and prayed a modified liturgy of the word, followed by a spontaneous homily of questions and reflections on the day's Gospel.

I realized that my daughters' insistence on "playing church" evinced two vital intuitions. First, they felt deservingly entitled to active, embodied participation in their faith. For them, it wasn't enough to watch Mass. They wanted to *do* church. Second, their identities as Christians had been formed almost entirely through participation in the life of our parish. They had never attended religious education classes, and their typical behavior during Mass led me to question whether they were paying attention at all. Yet neither my husband nor I taught them how to set up a home altar or instructed them to begin our service with a procession. We were stunned by the insightful questions they asked during our homily, often connecting ideas they heard in Scripture to contemporary situations of injustice. They had been catechized by their inclusion in the ritual life of our parish community.

My family's pandemic realization is at the foundation of the 2020 *Directory for Catechesis* (henceforth, *Directory*): we are formed by and for life in the community of the Church. While we often conceive of catechesis as direct instruction by a trained catechist, the *Directory* emphasizes that catechesis is also an integral process that occurs through a believer's immersion in the sacramental and social worlds of their ecclesial communities. Catholics locate their baptismal belonging within many different, intersecting communities. The *Directory* names several: the diocese, referred to as the "particular church" (§ 293-297), apostolic communities and ecclesial movements (§ 304-308), and Catholic schools (§ 309-318). Other communities form us, too: Catholic colleges and universities, campus ministries, service programs, digital spaces, and myriad others. We also learn the faith through the ordinary rhythms and relationships of everyday life, what Latinx theologians call *lo cotidiano*: through songs and stories, dinnertime conversations and familial practices and ancestral memories.[1]

In this chapter, I explore catechetical dimensions of perhaps our most ubiquitous and unassuming form of ecclesial community: the parish. According to the *Directory*, "Parishes manifest the face of the

[1] See Natalia Imperatori-Lee, *Cuéntame: Narrative in the Ecclesial Present* (Maryknoll, NY: Orbis, 2018).

people of God who opens himself to all, without preference of persons. They are 'the usual place in which the faith is born and in which it grows. [They] constitute, therefore, a very adequate community space for the realization of the ministry of the Word at once as teaching, education and life experience" (§ 299). In the parish, we are formed *by* and *for* community. As a community of difference, the parish is also where we live into the church as a *polyhedral* and *synodal* reality (§ 321). In the process of catechesis, then, the parish becomes a school of communion and solidarity, where we are formed for participation in the life of a diverse church and world.

Who, What, and Where is the Parish?

The parish, the most local ecclesial community, is the Body of Christ made manifest in a particular territorial place. Theologian Karl Rahner, SJ, described the parish the place where the Church is concretely realized as an event in the celebration of the Eucharist.[2] Gathering as

---

2   Karl Rahner, "Theology of the Parish," in *The Parish: From Theology to Practice*, ed. Hugo Rahner (Westminster, MD: Newman Press, 1958), 28.

church, parishioners become a living sign of the Incarnation. The act of gathering for the celebration of the Eucharist gestures toward the eschatological fulfillment of Jesus' prayer in John's Gospel that "all may be one" (John 17:21). As a Eucharistic community, parishioners are "[bound] by charity" toward "solicitude for the poorest" (§ 298). As Augustine famously wrote, in the Eucharist we become that which we receive: the Body of Christ.

Parishes are also communities of difference. Today, almost 40% of U.S. parishes serve communities that are culturally, ethnically, and/or linguistically diverse.[3] Most are also diverse in other ways: ideologically, politically, generationally, and economically. In dioceses undergoing restructuring, community-in-difference results after parishes have been shut down and merged. Mergers often create a sense of disorientation for all involved, leading communities to ask, "Who are we now?" The *Directory* states that the parish "brings together the many human differences within its boundaries and merges

3 See Center for Applied Research in the Apostolate. Available at https://cara.georgetown.edu/

them into the universality of the church" (§ 299). Yet this notion of "merging" human differences must be approached critically. The *Directory* draws this quotation from Vatican II's *Decree on the Apostolate of the Laity* (§ 10), promulgated in 1965. Today, such "melting pot" language, which promotes an image of difference dissolved in a cauldron of uniformity, is not only outdated; it also conflicts with the church's catholicity, as Hosffman Ospino illustrates in his chapter in this collection. Parishes are more adequately understood as "communities of communities" (§ 301), wherein common baptism and parochial belonging in no way denies human difference.

It is important to observe that when we speak of the "parish," we refer not merely to the church building or its members but to the totality of the territorial space encompassed by a parish's boundaries. Like the family, the parish is not an island insulated from the struggles and realities of the community within which it is embedded. A parish church in the United States is part of a local network that includes other houses of worship, homes, schools, civic institutions, places of business, organizations, and more. To name the parish as a vital space of catechetical formation, then, is also to name the valuable role that the local community plays in forming us for life together. Cultivating an ethic of solidarity with the local community goes beyond volunteering at the nearby soup kitchen or shelter. These acts of charity are important, but the *Directory* invites us to think about this relationship more mutually. What can we learn about the Christian life from our neighbors, including those of other faiths? How can we witness to Christ's mercy and love among our neighbors? How, in the words of Pope Francis, can we respond to the Gospel call to become "neighbors without borders" (*Fratelli Tutti*, § 80)?

Bringing together these two realities —the Eucharistic basis of the parish and the thoroughgoing reality of difference that characterizes parish life— raises an important caution. We must take care not to regard the Sacraments as accomplishing the work of Christian formation and unity on their own. The Eucharist does not unilaterally undo social inequality; it does not dissolve divisions between persons and communities or create social solidarity or redress all forms of harm. Certainly, Catholics believe that the Eucharist draws us together in Christ. Yet we should not regard this statement of belief as evidence of "mission accomplished" with respect to community life. The Eucharist does not give us license to ignore the real and pervasive effects of racism, xenophobia, and other forms of division and exclusion on our parish communities. By contrast, partaking in the Sacrament should nourish our resolve to build communities of love and justice.

Catechesis by and for Community

Formed by Community: The Parish as Teacher
Catechesis is the work of the entire community. As the *Directory* reminds us, "The whole Christian community is responsible for catechesis, even if only some receive from the bishop the mandate of being catechists" (§ 296). Just as the whole Church—the people of God—is "the agent of evangelization... so too catechesis is an action for which the whole Church feels responsible" (§ 287). As Christians, we learn what it means to be Church most deeply from

the inside out. Much of this learning occurs indirectly, through immersion in the spiritual, theological, social, and aesthetic environments of our local ecclesial communities. Every dimension of parish life—even those we are least likely to consider pedagogical—communicates something about what it means to be church: a parish's artwork, architecture, and statuary; the accessibility of its entrances and altar; its administration structures, leadership practices, and resource allocation; its racial, cultural, and gender dynamics; the homily and prayers of the faithful and music; its announcements and practices of welcome. The adage is true: actions speak louder than words. Parishes form Christians not principally by their catechetical curricula, but by the practice of the community itself.

Just as our parishes form Christian imaginations, they can also *deform*. Indeed, religious instruction is only as credible as it is true to one's lived experience of the church in one's parish. If a person reads that the church is a universal family encompassing people of all races, languages, and cultures, yet her parish is curiously mono-racial, monolingual, and mono-cultural, which of these two realities speaks more loudly? If she learns that Scripture prioritizes the protection of migrants and foreigners, yet her pastor assiduously avoids any discussion of immigrant justice as a taboo "controversial topic," what will she take away about Catholic belief in the dignity of migrants? If she is taught that the Church believes in the protection of the unborn, but she notices that the lone woman on the parish's pastoral staff was not granted maternity leave after giving birth, what has she learned? As Steffano Montano suggests in his chapter in this collection, the church's particular silences on antiracism speak volumes. No human community is perfect. Yet taking seriously the *Directory*'s call to consider the community as an agent of catechesis should encourage us in efforts to work for parish structures that more closely image the charity and justice at the heart of the Kingdom of God. Such efforts are never in vain.

Why is this recognition of the parish's catechetical character so important? As Catholics, we are often reminded that the family is the primary educator.

Without diminishing the role of the family, the *Directory's* vision of the community-as-catechist poses an implicit corrective to certain problems that arise in an overemphasis on the family's primacy. In a U.S. context, prioritizing the nuclear family often intersects with a harmful ethos of individualism, wherein supporting the common good is positioned as a threat to a family's ability to preserve its own advantages, security, and needs. This individualist paradigm portrays the opportunity to enjoy a life of dignity and happiness as a zero-sum game at which only some can succeed. Familial individualism is also miserable for families themselves. Individualism isolates families from one another, leading to loneliness, desperation, and a lack of social connection. We know that "it takes a village to raise a family," but more often, our social and ecclesial structures tell us, "every family for itself." The family may be a child's primary educator, but it is far from their only one. The Church, the *Directory* tells us, is a "family of families" (§ 137). The family is part of a relational network, not as an island unto itself.

Formed for Community: The Parish as Locus of the Christian Life

Just as believers are formed *by* the community, so too are they formed *for* community. The work of catechesis is governed by the *criterion of ecclesiality* (§ 176). "Faith is necessarily ecclesial," Pope Francis writes in the encyclical *Lumen Fidei*. "It is professed from within the body of Christ as a concrete communion of believers" (§ 22). For this reason, a litmus test of the adequacy of any catechetical model is the extent to which it forms believers into a life of faith practiced concretely in community. In the words of the *Directory*, "Catechesis initiates believers into the mystery of communion as lived, not only in relationship with the Father through Christ in the Spirit, but also in the community of believers through the work of the same Spirit. In educating for communion, catechesis educates for living in the Church and as the Church" (§ 176).

The ecclesial orientation of catechesis matters. Catechesis forms Christian believers in holiness. But holiness is not a solo endeavor. As theologian Elizabeth Johnson observes, in Scripture, the notion of sanctity is not generally used to describe an individual's moral status. Rather, it denotes "a consecration of [the people's] very being."[4] Individualistic notions of sanctity too often view holiness as designation for a heroically pious, solitary person—something that distinguishes one *from* the community. Vatican II's image of the church as the people of God (*Lumen Gentium*, Chapter II) reoriented holiness toward its relational roots. The church is a community of memory whereby we are formed by the love and wisdom of those who have preceded us in faith: apostles and martyrs, saints and theologians, church mothers and fathers, and our own beloved ancestors.

In *Gaudete et Exsultate* (2018), Pope Francis explains this idea compellingly:

> The Holy Spirit bestows holiness in abundance among God's holy and faithful people, for "it has pleased God to make men and women holy and to save them, not as individuals without any bond

[4] Elizabeth A. Johnson, *Friends of God and Prophets: A Feminist Theological Reading of the Communion of Saints* (New York, NY: Continuum, 1998), 58.

between them, but rather as a people who might acknowledge him in truth and serve him in holiness" (LG 9). In salvation history, the Lord saved one people. We are never completely ourselves unless we belong to a people. That is why no one is saved alone, as an isolated individual. Rather, God draws us to himself, taking into account the complex fabric of interpersonal relationships present in a human community. God wanted to enter into the life and history of a people (§ 6).

Peoplehood is a mark of the church's holiness. The church is holy to the extent that it is a people upholding one another in fidelity to God.

Needed Developments

The *Directory*'s vision of the communal nature and telos of catechesis provides a compelling vantage point from which to consider its relationship to catechesis. We can view the parish as a school of solidarity and communion—a place in and by which we are catechized for life in a diverse church. This recognition raises several needed developments:

Ritual as the Foundation

Catechesis is not primarily about communicating content but rather about forming Christians into a way of being. In this work, ritual—both in the liturgy and beyond—plays a fundamental role. This insight, echoed by Timothy O'Malley in his chapter in this collection, arrived in my living room at the beginning of the pandemic! Ritual forms our imaginations and desires. As embodied practice, ritual gives us ways of acting together meaningfully, even in the context of significant difference. In short, the Christian life is not a class exam: we *practice* our faith. A goal of catechesis, then, must be to empower individuals and families to practice a life of prayer, Christian witness, and solidarity in their homes and neighborhoods.

Structures of Accompaniment

As noted, the catechetical process often treats families as islands. Within most U.S. parishes, few structures exist to help families bond with one another. Strengthening relationships among families—perhaps through small groups, catechetical models geared specifically toward families with young children, babysitting co-ops and playgroups, and social celebrations—has myriad benefits. It gives children the opportunity to witness and participate in the faith practices of families other than their own, and it gives adults the opportunity for faith-filled friendships during a season of life in which the ability to sustain spiritual practices can be difficult. This, too, was a lesson my family learned during the pandemic. Like many, we joined with two other families to form a "pod." Though we initially did this so that our children would have playmates while schools were remote, we soon discovered the joys of praying together. We hosted a prayer service for the Feast of St. Francis in our backyard and Advent Lessons and Carols in our living room. This small community became integral to the survival of our faith and sanity during a time of great uncertainty.

Intergenerational Approaches
Catechetical leaders have long called for more integral approaches to catechesis. Yet while some parishes have experimented with whole-family

models, catechesis remains generationally segmented: religious education classes for children, youth group for teens, topical faith formation opportunities for adults, and so on. Generational segmentation in catechesis not only overlooks particular age groups; it also robs the faithful of opportunities to learn from one another. Supplementing generationally specific catechetical programs by cultivating spaces and practices of intergenerational community can help. In this respect (and many others), predominately Euro-American parishes have much to learn from Hispanic/Latinx communities, wherein religious education is often an intergenerational and communal endeavor. Ultimately, the *Directory* calls us to view catechesis not as a series of programs but as the orienting basis of the whole community.

An End to White Supremacy and Xenophobia.
Racism and discrimination are among the greatest sources of division in the church. As Steffano Montano and Lakisha Lockheart affirm in their chapters in this collection, the possibility of

solidarity is undermined by structures and attitudes that privilege white, Euro-American faith expressions and liturgical practices. Too often, imbalances of power, resources, leadership, and access to parish facilities lead to egregious disparities among cultural sub-communities. Uninterrogated racial biases and anti-immigrant nationalism on the part of parishioners, pastoral ministers, and clergy further militate against belonging. Until parishes commit to rooting out white supremacy, xenophobia, and discrimination in all forms, they will continue to form Christians afflicted by diseased understandings of human worth.

In closing, as my family learned during the pandemic, we are catechized in ways we often hardly realize by our participation in community. As the primary locus of liturgical and sacramental practice, and as the space in which the *Directory*'s call for ecclesially-oriented catechesis is manifested, the parish is of fundamental importance. Taking seriously the pedagogical quality of every dimension of parish life encourages us in the work of cultivating communities grounded in Gospel charity, justice, joy, and belonging.

Questions for Conversation:
1. In what ways have you been formed in faith by the communities to which you belong?
2. What do you see as your parish's greatest strengths as a catechetical community, a school of solidarity and communion? Where do you perceive areas for growth?

Recommended Readings:
Pope Francis. *Fratelli Tutti*, On Fraternity and Social Friendship (2020)

Brett Hoover. *The Shared Parish: Latinos, Anglos, and the Future of U.S. Catholicism.* New York, NY: NYU Press, 2014.
Natalia Imperatori-Lee. *Cuéntame: Narrative in the Ecclesial Present.* Maryknoll, NY: Orbis, 2018.

12

Lost in Cultural Translation:
A Roadmap for Catechesis in a Culturally Diverse Church

Hosffman Ospino

A few years ago, I traveled to Berlin for a meeting of religious education researchers. I knew no German, although I had learned a couple of words that I figured would help me through my stay: *Ja* and *Nein* (yes and no). All went well at the airport, the hotel and my meeting, mostly because people there also spoke English and Spanish, two languages in which I am fluent. Things got interesting when participants in the meeting split into smaller groups to explore the local culture and I, audaciously, chose to go with a group of mostly German-speakers.

We went to dinner at a local restaurant. Everyone there communicated in German, so I figured that it was time for some cultural baptism by immersion, and perhaps practice my limited vocabulary. My plan was that when someone said something and I did not understand, I would take a risk and say, *"ja."* The next time, I would likely say, *"nein."* My calculation was that I could be right or wrong only half of the time. A waiter came and said something. I looked puzzled, yet enthusiastically said, *"ja!"* A few minutes later, something that looked like raw meat was in front of me. I had never eaten a similar dish—and I always eat my meat well done! I found someone who spoke English and told her that what was on my dish looked like raw meat. She said, "Well, of course, it's *Mett.*" The waiter came back later and said something again. I stuck to my strategy and this time, cautiously, said *"nein."* My local interpreter asked, "You do not want to eat anything for dinner?" I was lost in translation. I needed help. We had a great evening, but I could not have survived on my own.

Cultural Diversity: Challenge and Opportunity

Anecdotes about being lost in translation tend to be humorous, usually after the fact. We all can tell similar stories: a trip to another country, learning a new language, meeting someone who comes from a different culture, etc. In many cases, it is more than fine to make mistakes. After all, we learn from these.

We can try again, and again. However, that may not always be possible. Being lost in translation can be risky. Someone may lose something. We may find ourselves in difficult or even life-threatening situations. We may not be able to try things again.

Catholics in the United States do not need to travel overseas or leave the immediacy of our parishes to experience cultural and linguistic diversity. About 40 % of all Catholic parishes in the country celebrate services in a language other than English, and have large contingents of parishioners who most likely were born in another country. If you are in your sixties, you may remember a time when most Catholics in the U.S. (about 90%) self-identified as Euro-American, white. That is not the case any longer. About 45% of all U.S. Catholics and nearly 60% of Catholics under 18 are Hispanic. About 5% are Asian, 3.9% Black—including African Americans and immigrants from Africa and the Caribbean—and slightly less than 1% Native American. While the median age of white Catholics is 55, it is only 30 for all Hispanics, 34 for all Black people and 37 for all Asians in our country. This gives us a sense of who is coming to our catechetical programs, who should be attending our Catholic schools, the cultural background of most Catholic children and youth, and why we all need to take cultural diversity seriously.

The rich diversity of cultures and experiences that defines the U.S. Catholic experience in the third decade of the twenty-first century is fascinating. Such cultural diversity affords us the opportunity to learn about the many catholicisms that coexist in our faith communities. The various cultural groups that make up the U.S. Catholic body often congregate in parishes with so called ethnic ministries, evoking the national parishes of old, yet most of the time their practice of the faith transcends parish boundaries and structures. There is much to appreciate about how Catholics from different cultural backgrounds appropriate, interpret, celebrate and pass on the faith. Yet, catechizing amidst cultural diversity is not always easy. It requires intercultural competencies that are not necessarily instinctive. We must develop these with intentionality. It may require a new type of catechist and a fresher awareness about how faith and culture interact.

In 2020, the Pontifical Council for Promoting New Evangelization released the new *Directory for Catechesis* (henceforth, *Directory*). It is the third of its kind, after the 1971 and 1997 versions. The *Directory* provides an inspiring framework to plan and organize catechesis in the Catholic world. It reminds us with utmost clarity that "Communion with Jesus Christ, who died and rose again, who is living and always present, is the ultimate end of all ecclesial action and therefore of catechesis as well" (§ 426). The aim is clear.

In our particular context, all catechetical efforts must foster communion with Jesus Christ amidst cultural diversity. This means that we must factor in respect for differences, pedagogical sensitivities and language awareness, among other realities associated with culture, as we envision our catechetical experiences. We must remember that the vast majority of Catholics engage in formal catechetical learning only for brief periods in their lives, especially during their younger years or around the time of receiving the sacraments. If we do not engage the young when they are with us, they may not return later. Immigrants and underrepresented groups may never return to a parish, a school or a faith formation group if they perceive that they are not welcomed and valued. We must catechize well. We may not have another chance.

What the New Directory for Catechesis Says —and Does Not Say—About Culture

Culture is one of those words that catechetical leaders, experts and practitioners toss around quite loosely. There are libraries dedicated to the question of faith and culture, and many of the works are written from a Catholic perspective. The *Directory* uses the term culture much more than its predecessors do. This is more evident in the original version of the document in Italian. Culture and its cognates appear in the *Directory* about 259 times, 36 of these associated to "inculturation; 202 times in the *General Directory for Catechesis* (1997), 47 in association to inculturation. Culture and its cognates appear only 37 times in the *General Catechetical Directory* (1971), never using the term inculturation.

We learn three things from this expanding use of the term culture. One, Catholics are growing more comfortable using the category to name how we receive, interpret and pass on the faith. Two, the more we articulate our reflection on evangelization and catechesis in missionary language, the more attention we pay to conversations about culture. Three, the *Directory* has been significantly influenced by Pope Francis' thoughts on evangelization and culture.

The *Directory* does not necessarily provide a formal definition of culture. The closest it comes to doing so is when it vaguely refers to "culture as a hermeneutic setting for the faith" (§ 396). The 1997 *General Directory for Catechesis*, in a footnote, referred its readers to Vatican II's *Gaudium et Spes*, § 59, to explain how it understood culture. One can safely assume that the invitation in the new *Directory* remains (cf. § 331). The wide and sometimes unclear use of the word culture in the *Directory* offers a potpourri of possibilities that is both inspiring and vexing. For instance, the *Directory* speaks of "culture of encounter" (§§ 6, 104), "today's culture" (§ 42), "the prevailing culture" (§ 46), "Christian culture" (§ 102), "culture of inclusion" (§ 271), "farming culture" (§ 330), "traditional local cultures" (§ 331), "cultures of indigenous peoples" (§

334), "culture of the lowly" (§ 336), "culture of death" (§ 379), "cultural ecology" (§ 383), "culture of fraternity" (§ 388), "global culture" (§ 331), "digital culture" (§ 359), etc.

The *Directory* technically argues that catechesis is to lead believers into the cultivation of cultural frameworks —when they facilitate evangelization— or confront them —when they get in the way of Christ. It is hard to disagree with the invitation. However, the order is tall! What does exactly a "culture of inclusion" mean? No definition. In fact, the document struggles with the idea of inclusion at its most basic level when the original Italian ironically fails to use gender inclusive language— a stylistic decision kept in other translations, including Spanish and there is little or no reference to the rich catechetical traditions and realities of African and Asian Catholics.

Cultural Plurality

Problematic is also the use of the category "Christian culture," which one encounters regularly in church documents. The *Directory* assumes the existence of a Christian culture that is "new and original," characterized by an "evangelical style;" one that "over the course of the centuries has produced true masterpieces in all branches of knowledge" (§ 102). One of the most important accomplishments of that Christian culture, according to the *Directory*, is the preservation of "Greek philosophy and Roman jurisprudence" (§ 104). In an almost romantic way, the *Directory* says that this culture became a heritage that has influenced nearly every realm of human existence, and thus catechesis needs to continue to spread it (§ 105). If one reads between the lines, the *Directory* seems to be making a tacit endorsement of the glorious days of European Christendom. No one can deny the contributions of this particular heritage, but presenting it uncritically without reference to centuries of colonialism, violence, racism, machismo, debasement of other cultures—often misreading the Gospel to justify these horrors—does not bring the *Directory* up to date with the growing sensibilities many Catholics share in our day, especially the younger generations.

In its treatment of cultural realities, the *Directory* excels in bringing awareness to the pluralistic nature of human experience in the twenty-first century. I believe that this is one of its most important contributions. To state the obvious: this is the twenty-first century, not the early twentieth or the nineteenth. This should serve as a warning to Catholic catechetical leaders who instead of looking forward and *"en salida"* (going forth), dwell in sacristies and temples on reminiscences about glorified pasts. The *Directory* identifies the rise of digital culture and globalization as likely the two most ground-shaking cultural phenomena of our time (cf. *Directory*'s preface). Along these realities, the *Directory* also reminds catechists that urban realities define the lives of perhaps most Catholics in our day (§§ 326-328). Borders and identities shift constantly as immigrants and refugees cross them searching for new homes and faith communities that welcome them. They look for local communities that embrace them and together discern the Gospel, build church and find ways to pass on the faith to the next generations (§§ 273-278). All these realities, among others, point to the emergence of new ways of being human. A crown jewel insight in the *Directory*, in reference to the influence of technology, is the observation that we are witnessing a "genuine anthropological transformation" (§ 362). It is the birth of a new self and new ways of being Christian in the world. I wish the *Directory* had expanded this anthropological analysis to the rest of the cultural phenomena it names. Whether the focus is technology, globalization, immigration, cultural plurality, urban ministry, discernment of identities, religion in the public square, etc., we are in the midst of "a true anthropological revolution" (§ 46).

Inculturation and Its Limits
There is no doubt that the *Directory* is especially fond of the category inculturation. The term appears many times throughout the document and actually gets its own chapter (Chapter X). The section is short, rather unimpressive and lacking in novelty. Catholics have been using the term inculturation for nearly half a century. It rests on the incarnational paradigm: just as the Word becomes flesh and assumes a fallen humanity to redeem it, so does the Gospel—received, interpreted and shared—transforms culture(s). If the

goal is something that may resemble a "Christian culture," perhaps a chimera within the realm of history considering that sin and evil remain part of our existential experience, there is value in inculturation as an eschatological promise. In other words, inculturation is as a permanent, yet unfinished project for the pilgrim church (cf. §§ 172, 287). The *Directory* invites catechetical leaders, starting with bishops (§ 114), to make every effort possible to inculturate the faith. Catechesis does this while echoing the process of evangelization (§§ 42-47). The *Directory* proposes the catechumenate as a model of inculturation (§ 64). In particular, local catechisms are ideal resources to reflect about inculturation efforts in catechesis since they address particular questions, concerns and realities in local communities (§ 401).

What the *Directory* does not do, which is rather unfortunate, is to address the limitations of inculturation and then expand the Catholic imagination about how faith and culture(s) interact in a pluralistic world. Inculturation makes it sound too easy: a godless culture, holding some seeds of the

Word within (§ 355), awaits for the Gospel. The Gospel (i.e., usually associated with an institution, the Christian Bible or a set of predefined doctrines) comes, engages, purifies and perfects that culture. Something new emerges: a Christian culture? If so, as a human enterprise, it is a mixture of grace and sin considering our limitations. Living in a culturally pluralistic context like the U.S. society seems to beg for much more. So does living in pluralistic regions like Asia and Africa.

A growing body of literature on intercultural theory holds promise. Interculturalism affirms the autonomy of cultures as a starting point and sets the stage for a dialogue of mutuality. The Gospel, without negotiating its claims to truth and universal value, enters into such dialogue as a partner. Partners agree mutually on the rules of engagement in light of the context and expected goals. Biases and prejudices are named—if necessary denounced—at the outset. Power differences require correction and balancing. The initial outcomes of intercultural dialogue may not be clear until the process is long in motion. Catholics involved in ecumenical and interreligious dialogue have much to share about these intercultural conversations. For more on dialogue, see Jane Regan's chapter in this collection. Catechesis in diverse contexts requires the engagement of intercultural pedagogies. It is time for Catholicism to engage in fresher conversation about how faith and culture relate in a pluralistic world as well as the type of catechesis that such a conversation will demand. I share some seminal thoughts about this in my book *Interculturalism and Catechesis: A Catechist's Guide to Responding to Cultural Diversity*. Perhaps the next directory for catechesis will be more venturous in this regard.

Toward a Culturally Responsive Catechesis

The *Directory's* eclectic treatment of culture and its overreliance on an uncritical use of inculturation do not seem sufficient to address the complex catechetical realities of the U.S. culturally diverse Catholic context. I say this for three reasons. One, ours remains a profoundly religious nation whose understanding of Christianity—and Catholicism within it—fluctuates between glimpses of orthodoxy and de facto heresy as it evolves alongside the larger American sociopolitical project. Two, methodological and interpretive simplifications about faith and culture fail to acknowledge the coexistence of multiple ways of being Catholic shaped by racial, ethnic, migratory, linguistic, social, generational and even ideological dynamics that simultaneously influence and question one another in our faith communities. Three, Catholics in the United States in the twenty-first century are permanently adapting, sometimes stumbling, to make a credible case for Jesus Christ amidst myriad options that claim to offer religious meaning to our own people, especially the young. We do this while wrestling with external challenges such as secularization and self-inflicted wounds like the clerical sexual abuse scandals of recent decades.

It will fall upon the team drafting the national directory for catechesis, the textbooks and other catechetical guides that follow the 2020 *Directory* to provide a more dynamic assessment of the relationship between catechesis and culture in light of the complexity of our local reality. We need to envision a good culturally responsive catechesis that brings Catholics of all cultural backgrounds in the U.S. into communion with Jesus Christ without ignoring who we are, or the context where we live. The task is urgent and complex. A yes-or-no approach that calculates minimum risk cannot be acceptable. We cannot afford to be lost in translation. Simplistic approaches to cultural diversity, the spiritualization of catechesis and attempts to homogenize Catholic life and practice may lead to more disaffiliation.

Catechetical leaders particularly in dioceses and parishes who accept the challenge to develop culturally responsive catechetical experiences while imagining wider horizons for faith formation will need to make at least three commitments:

Dedicate resources to understand well the epochal change in which we are living (cf. *Directory*, §§ 38, 319). Catechesis in the United States occurs in the midst of a complex and multifaceted reality. In the words of the *Directory*, this heterogeneous reality "needs to be interpreted in such a way that its *polyhiedral* character may be grasped and every aspect may preserve its validity and uniqueness while still in its intricate relationship to the whole" (§ 321).

Empower particular communities to be active agents of the catechetical experience. Catechesis in the U.S. depends too much on centralized systems (e.g., parish weekly programs, schools) that often reflect the pedagogical commitments and interests of predominant groups. We must place catechesis in the hands of families (§ 124), the young with their capacity to dream and renew (§ 244), the poor (§ 387), immigrants (§ 275), and marginalized persons and communities (§ 279), among others. It is time to acknowledge that we may need help from those voices that our catechetical efforts may have ignored but are there and perhaps know more.

Cultivate a new generation of catechists with real expertise in reading the signs of times (cf. §§ 5, 319), catechists who know themselves as "called to understand human beings in the concrete and in the sociocultural context in which they live" (§ 146). For that, they must learn to "take into serious consideration the rapidity of social change and the plurality of cultures, with the challenges that stem from this" (§ 130). They should undergo a formation that gives them what they need to *"prepare an itinerary of faith* that consists in considering socio-cultural circumstances (§ 149c). Our U.S. pluralistic context needs catechists who are true *gente puente* (bridge people) and cultural brokers.

Questions for Conversation:
1. In what ways does the *Directory for Catechesis*' reminder that we live in a profoundly pluralistic world invite you be mindful about questions of culture, race and language when you catechize?
2. Aware of the many cultural realities that shape the lives of Catholics in our day, what do you need to be a *bridge person* or *cultural broker* in your faith community, and help others to be likewise?

Recommended Readings:
Hosffman Ospino. *Interculturalism and Catechesis: A Catechist's Guide to Responding to Cultural Diversity.* New Haven, CT: Twenty-Third Publications, 2017.

Pope Francis. *Evangelii Gaudium*, On the Proclamation of the Gospel in Today's World (2013)

United States Conference of Catholic Bishops. Secretariat for Cultural Diversity in the Church, *Building Intercultural Competence for Ministers*. Washington, D.C.: USCCB, 2012.

Contributors

Susan Bigelow Reynolds, PhD is Assistant Professor of Catholic Studies at Candler School of Theology at Emory University in Atlanta, GA. Her first book, an ecclesiological and ethnographic examination of intercultural solidarity and ritual in U.S. parish life, will be published by Fordham University Press in 2022. She has a decade of experience in Catholic education, parish ministry, and liturgical music ministry. She and her husband are the grateful parents of three young daughters.

Thomas H. Groome is Professor of Theology and Religious Education at Boston College School of Theology and Ministry. He received a doctorate in Theology and Education from Columbia University/Union Theological Seminary. Author of numerous books on religious education and faith formation, including the influential *Sharing Faith: A Comprehensive Approach to Religious Education and Pastoral Ministry. The Way of Shared Praxis* (Harper Collins, 1991). His most recent works are *Faith for the Heart* (Paulist Press, 2019) and *What Makes Education Catholic: Its Spiritual Foundations* (Orbis, 2021).

Lakisha R. Lockhart, PhD is Assistant Professor of Practical Theology at Chicago Theological Seminary and Executive Secretary of the Religious Education Association. She also serves as a consultant for the Campus Ministry Theological Exploration of Vocation Initiative with the Forum for Theological Exploration on behalf of the Lilly Endowment, Inc. This playful womanist scholar actively advocates for the usage of the body as a locus for doing theology through embodied and playful pedagogical practices.

Patrick Manning, PhD is Assistant Professor of Pastoral Theology and Chair of the Department of Pastoral Theology at Immaculate Conception Seminary School of Theology at Seton Hall University. With a background in both Catholic parishes and schools, he is a frequent workshop facilitator and presenter on topics related to catechesis and theological education. He has authored numerous catechetical works and resources including *Converting the Imagination: Teaching to Recover Jesus' Vision for Fullness of Life* (Pickwick, 2020).

Theresa A. O'Keefe, PhD is Associate Professor at Boston College School of Theology and Ministry. Dr. O'Keefe's research, writing, and teaching focus on youth and young adult faith. Recognizing that young people are formed in diverse settings, she looks to how Catholic parishes, secondary schools, or universities best contribute to their formation. Her award-winning book is *Navigating toward Adulthood: A Theology of Ministry with Adolescents* (Paulist Press, 2018).

Hosffman Ospino, PhD is Associate Professor of Theology and Religious Education at Boston College School of Theology and Ministry where he also chairs the Department of Religious Education and Pastoral Ministry (DREPM). His research focuses on the relationship between faith and culture, and how that conversation shapes catechesis, theological education and ministerial activity in culturally diverse contexts. He has authored and edited more than a dozen books on ministry and catechesis.

Jane E. Regan, PhD is Associate Professor of Theology and Religious Education at Boston College School of Theology and Ministry. Dr. Regan's research, writing, and teaching focus on adult faith formation and communities of practice. In her most recent book, *Where Two or Three Are Gathered: Transforming the Parish Through Communities of Practice* (Paulist Press, 2016), she examines the importance of conversation to the faith formation and the life of the parish.

Nat Samuel, PhD is Assistant Professor of Liberation Theology at the Institute of Pastoral Studies, Loyola University Chicago where he teaches classes in Liberation Theology, Social Justice, Catholic Social Ethics, and Theology and Political Economy. His research interests include narrative approaches to educating for justice and Caribbean theologies of liberation. He has many years of experience with ministry in the RCIA program, and in leading parish conversations on issues of faith and justice.

Susanna Singer, PhD retired in July 2020 as Associate Professor of Ministry Development and Associate Academic Dean at Church Divinity School of the Pacific, where she had served on the faculty for fifteen years. She holds an M.Div. from Church Divinity School of the Pacific, and an M.A. in English Literature from the University of Cambridge. She has been an Episcopal priest for thirty years, and previously served as Education Coordinator for the Diocese of California and Canon Liturgist and Educator at Grace Cathedral, San Francisco.

Daniella Zsupan-Jerome, PhD is Director of Ministry Formation and Field Education at St John's University School of Theology in Collegeville MN. Her research explores the intersection of social communication, digital culture, and pastoral theology. She has served as a consultant to the United States Conference of Catholic Bishops' Committee on Communications and as an educational consultant to the Catholic Media Association. Her major publications include: *Connected Toward Communion: The Church and Social*

Communication in the Digital Age (Liturgical Press, 2014); *Evangelization and Catechesis: Echoing the Good News Through the Documents of the Church* (Twenty-Third Publications, 2017); *Authority and Leadership: Values, Religion, Media* (co-editor, Blanquerna, 2017).

www.ingramcontent.com/pod-product-compliance
Lightning Source LLC
Chambersburg PA
CBHW032021230426
43671CB00005B/157